TOM SEAVER AND ME

TOM SEAVER AND ME

Pat Jordan

Post Hill
PRESS

A POST HILL PRESS BOOK
ISBN: 978-1-64293-461-8
ISBN (eBook): 978-1-64293-462-5

Tom Seaver and Me
© 2020 by Pat Jordan
All Rights Reserved

Interior design and layout by Sarah Heneghan, sarah-heneghan.com

This is a work of nonfiction. All people, locations, events, and situations are portrayed to the best of the author's memory.

Post Hill Press
New York • Nashville
posthillpress.com

Published in the United States of America

For Tom, who is my idol, as, of course, I am his.

Prologue

Tom Seaver and I were friends for forty-five years. Not the best of friends. Not intimate friends... Our wives going shopping together into Manhattan. Tom and I staying behind at his farmhouse in Greenwich, watching a baseball game on TV in his family room. Our wives returning late in the afternoon, laughing gaily, swinging their shopping bags from Saks and Bloomingdale's in the kitchen where Tom and I are preparing dinner. Tom and I looking at them, their bags, then each other, rolling our eyes, Tom saying, "This is gonna cost us, big time."

We didn't have "the Seavers" over for dinner, nor did they have "the Jordans" over for dinner. We didn't take vacations together like close couples do.... A winter week in the Bahamas. Nancy and Susie sunbathing on the beach, matching, beautiful, tanned blondes. Tom and I watching them from a tiki bar in the sand, looking at each other, smiling at our good fortune, then drinking our beers, smoking our cigars, talking baseball, pitching mostly. At sunset, after showers, all of us meeting for drinks at the resort's bar, and then a late-night dinner at a table by the pool under the stars like diamonds on black velvet, the moonlight slashes of white on the black ocean. The four of us, talking, laughing, friends.

Susie and Nancy never met. It was only Tom and I who were friends. When he was pitching for the New York Mets and the Cincinnati Reds in the '70s and '80s, we would talk on the phone maybe once a month. He was famous then. The most celebrated athlete in the country. Everyone wanted his time. I didn't want to bother him. But sometimes I couldn't control myself. I'd be sitting on the edge of my sofa in the living room, leaning toward the TV, watching him pitch a night game on television. He'd throw a pitch, I'd moan, "For crissakes, Tom!" I had to repress my urge to call him after the game in his hotel room in St. Louis, or LA, or Frisco. It was a struggle. But I would wait until the next morning before I called him.

"Tom, it's me."

"What do you want?"

"I saw you pitch last night."

"And?"

"You're hanging your curveball."

"Tell me something I don't know."

"You're not dropping your left shoulder and elevating your right shoulder on the curve."

"Really? You think so?"

"Absolutely."

"What the fuck do you know?"

"I know how to throw a fucking curveball is what I know."

When we became old men, in our late sixties, I called him less frequently, a few times a year. We'd talk about our quiet lives now, our dogs, our pleasure in cooking, but never baseball. "That part's over," Tom said. He lived with Nancy and his dogs in seclusion on a mountaintop in the picturesque Napa Valley wine country, where he had a small vineyard. He woke every morning at 4:00 a.m. to prune his vines. I lived in seclusion with Susie and our dogs in a tiny town in northwestern South Carolina. A world away from Fort Lauderdale Beach, where we'd lived for almost thirty years. I described it to my

Fort Lauderdale friends as "a little bit old, a little bit worn, a little bit out of the way. Perfect." When they visited us, I drove them around the town square over the lumpy, two-hundred-year-old brick street, past the decaying two-story brick buildings, the Confederate soldier statue on the center green, the horse fountain, the churches at all four corners, and then, in a blink, we were out of town, and as far as the eye could see nothing but rolling farmland. My friends shook their heads in disbelief and said, "Jesus! This is East Bumfuck nowhere." I shrugged, told them, "Yeah, well, it's not Fort Liquordale, but it'll do."

Like Tom, I woke at 4:00 a.m. to work. I wrote every day at my desk.

One late afternoon, Napa Valley time, I called Tom to ask him for a favor.

"Tom, it's me."

"What do you want?"

"Are you busy?"

"I'm working. I'm putting my babies to sleep for the night."

"You have more kids?"

"My grapes."

"Your grapes?"

"They're my babies."

"Jesus, Tom. You gotta get a life."

"You mean like *yours*? You still spending your days in an empty room? Staring at a blank piece of paper in a typewriter?" He laughed. "You call that a life?"

"It's a blank screen. I write on a computer now."

"Same thing."

"You talk to grapes, for crissakes."

"I told you, they're my babies."

"Do they talk back?"

"Of course."

"What do they say?"

"This morning they warned me a pain in the ass would call. 'Be warned!' they said. Now what do you want?"

"I need a favor."

"Again?" The last and only other favor I'd asked of Tom was in the late '80s. Susie and I were broke in Fort Lauderdale, after I'd given my ex-wife the house, the car, and a huge alimony in the divorce. We lived in a 450-square-foot apartment on a canal. We could barely pay the $500-a-month rent. We cut out coupons from the Sunday newspaper supplements so we could buy cans of Blue Bird tuna for 9 cents. If we were flush, we went to bars on the Intracoastal and ordered beers. Then we ate their happy-hour buffet for our dinner. Chicken wings. Chow mein. BBQ ribs. Burritos. Carrots and celery stalks with blue cheese dressing. We left two dollars for the beers and a dollar tip. When our rusted, old Alfa Romeo was totaled outside our apartment at 3:00 a.m. by a drunk driver, we pedaled around town on a beach cruiser bike. We stole a T-bone steak from Winn-Dixie. Susie sat on the handlebars of our beach cruiser, clutching the steak to her chest, kicking her legs, while I pedaled furiously back to our apartment.

Finally, I called an editor friend at *People* magazine, then I called Tom. I told him *People* wanted me to write a story about him and Nancy approaching retirement. He said, "*People*? With photos? Me and Nancy in a hot tub sipping champagne? No fucking way." I said, "No hot tub. I guarantee it." Silence. I waited. Finally, I said, "I need the money." Tom said, "When do you want to do it?"

Now, almost twenty years later, I needed another favor. So I told him a story. My daughter hadn't spoken to me in twenty years because of the divorce from her mother, my first wife. That's how kids see it when their parents divorce. "The Divorce." As if it's the only one. To them it is, the only one that matters.

"So now my grandson I've never met is asking about me," I told Tom. "He's eight and he loves baseball. He wants to know about his grandfather who was a baseball player once. My daughter dropped me a note to tell me this."

"So what can I do?"

"My daughter said it would mean a lot to my grandson if I could get him a baseball player's autograph. I told her I don't know any guys playing today. I haven't been in a clubhouse for years."

"Me, too," Tom said. "Been there, done that."

"Then I thought of you."

"Send me his name and address on a piece of paper and I'll send him something."

"I'll email the address."

"I don't have email."

"Then I'll fax it."

"I don't have a fax."

"Jeez, what are you, a recluse?"

"What do you think I should be doing? Playing in celebrity golf tournaments in Vegas?"

"I hope not."

"I tend my grapes, play with my dogs, and don't leave home unless it's to visit my daughters and grandkids."

"Me, too. I tell people I don't leave my house unless I get paid."

"Why should you?"

"I'd rather stay home with my wife and dogs. I have six."

"Wives?"

"No. Only two. One's an ex. Actually, I have only four dogs left. Two died over the last three years. That was rough. Rougher than my parents dying."

"Tell me about it." I asked him how Nancy was. He said, "The same."

"Is that good or bad?"

"You tell me."

I remembered Nancy from years ago. She often played the ditzy California blonde housewife of the superstar husband to deflect attention from herself. At first, I thought, "Nobody home." Then I got to know her. I saw her many times make Tom blush, splutter, speechless.

"Mostly good," I said. Then I asked him about his two Lab retrievers. He told me that they chased the deer and coyotes from his precious vines. I remembered his first dog I knew years ago. His name was Slider. Slider's long gone. I told Tom once, "You shoulda named him Curveball; you woulda won more games." Not the wise guy now, he said, "It always bothered me. I could never grasp the concept of the curveball."

I told Tom I'd mail him a note with my grandson's name and address. He said, "The minute it hits my desk, I'll have it in the mail the same day."

"I shudder to think what I'm gonna owe you for this."

"I'll think of something."

"How about this? I'll promise never again to remind you that I threw harder than you."

"In your dreams."

When I got off the phone, I wrote my grandson's name and address on a piece of paper, added a little note thanking Tom, and stuck it inside the cover of my latest book. I inscribed the book, "To Tom, who is my idol, as I am his." Then I FedExed it all to him.

A week later a little boy called my house. I picked up the phone to a voice that said, "This is Adam." I was momentarily confused until he said, "I'm your grandson." It sounded strange, "Grandson," from a little boy I'd never met. He thanked me for Tom's autograph. Tom had sent him a photo of himself in a Mets uniform, along with a note written across the photograph. It read, "Your grandfather, my friend, told me you're a future Hall of Famer. I hope you like this. Your friend, Tom Seaver."

I heard my grandson's voice saying, "Now I'm gonna have to root for the Mets, Grandpa, not the Phillies." I'd forgot that he lived in Philadelphia.

"The Mets are a better team, anyway," I said. Then I told him to get the photo laminated so it wouldn't get ripped. He said, "Mr. Seaver sent it already laminated."

When my grandson got off the phone, my daughter got on. I hadn't heard her voice in twenty years. But it sounded the same. Clipped. Judgmental. She thanked me for the autograph. "He won't put it down," she said. "He's afraid if he leaves the house someone will steal it." I laughed; she didn't. She said, "John's going to get it framed." It took me a split second to realize she meant my son-in-law I'd never met.

"Good," I said. "I'm glad it made him happy."

My daughter said, "He tells everyone his grandfather used to play baseball." She was silent for a moment; then she said, "He wants to see you."

"Well, come visit us," I said.

"We'll see." Enigmatic, like her mother. She said, "Goodbye," and hung up. I didn't expect her to call me "Dad."

The next afternoon the mailman delivered a letter from my grandson. In perfect printing, he had written, "Thanks Grandpa for getting me an autograph from Tom Seaver. It means a lot to me." Then he signed it, "To Grandpa, with love, Adam."

I also got a note from Tom, written on some Little League organization's stationary. It read, "Done!" I called him.

"What do you want now?" he bellowed over the noise of traffic in the background.

"Where are you?"

"I'm on the highway driving to my daughter's house for Christmas. She's got rug rats now." I remembered his daughter's name, Sarah. She was a cute little blonde rug rat herself when I knew her as a young child. Now she must be pushing forty.

I told Tom how thrilled my grandson was with "Mr. Seaver's" autographed photo. "He's getting it framed," I said, "for his bedroom wall."

"I know," Tom said. "He sent me a thank-you note." That was nice of my daughter, I thought. One of the many things I didn't know about her.

I said, "My grandson was very impressed that you referred to me as your friend." He didn't say anything. "I told my grandson, 'Actually, Adam, Mr. Seaver is grateful I consider him *my* friend.'" Tom actually harrumphed, like a character out of Dickens. Tom *was* Dickensian. Big, blustery, obvious. There was no deceit in Tom. For as long as I've known him, from his late twenties to his seventies, he has retained vestiges of a young boy's innocence.

"Did you read my book I sent you?" I asked.

"The first page."

"That interesting, huh? I should have sent you a little yellow ruler, too." Nothing. I was boring him with my sarcasm, as I often did. Tom is a literal man, with not much patience for a smart-ass writer. I said, "Did you like the inscription?"

"That's the same inscription you wrote on the previous book you sent me. Where's your fucking creativity?"

"No, it isn't."

"Yes, it is." We squabbled back and forth over the past, accusing each other of faded memories. I said, "You're just jealous because you're a washed-up old ballplayer and I'm still a young writer." Finally, he laughed.

"Talk about frustrated," Tom said. "You've never gotten over the fact that you're not me."

But I had, after thirty-five years. I just didn't tell him I had. I said, "You're the one who should be frustrated. Big fucking deal pitcher knowing I threw harder than you." I had already broken my promise to him in a week.

"You wish."

"Remember Terry Tata?" I said. "Spring training seventy-two. St. Pete, Al Lang Field, behind the batting cage. What'd Terry say?"

"That never happened," Tom said.

"Oh, yes it did. You just repressed it."

"Is that why you're in the Hall of Fame?"

"I still threw harder than you."

"Yeah, and between me and you we won three hundred and eleven games."

"Exactly! I tell everyone that."

After we hung up, I felt bad that I'd embarrassed Tom, again, by reminding him of my superior fastball. So to make him feel good, I sent him another note. I described for him a terrible argument Susie and I had one night in our early forties, before we got married. We were standing in the dark outside a restaurant alongside a commuter railroad track in Westport, screaming at each other. Susie had a glass of vodka in her hand, I had a glass of bourbon in mine. We stood about thirty feet apart, half the distance from a pitcher's mound to home plate. A train roared past us. In a frustrated rage, Susie threw her glass at me. It missed my head by six inches. I fired my glass at her. It missed her by six feet. She gave me a small smile as the train's roar receded in the distance. Still smiling, she said, "No wonder you never made the Bigs."

I thought Tom would like that story. He did. After he got my note he called me. "When am I gonna meet Susie?" he said. "I like her already."

⬟ ⬟ ⬟

We have a lot in common, Tom and me. In our seventies we're still vigorous, physical men, still in good shape, close to our playing weight, still competitive. We haven't changed much in over forty years. We still call each other "Big Guy." Tom still looks like Tom Seaver, with only flecks of gray in his sandy hair, maybe a little more fleshy, although he always had a pudgy face and chunky body. I, however, don't look much like myself of forty years ago, although my face is still angular and lean. My luxuriant black curls of my twenties and thirties turned to gray in my forties, then white in my fifties, and now are gone in my seventies. My once black pirate's beard is white. I look more like Hemingway than myself. I don't mind. I was seventy-three the last time Tom saw me. He said, "You got old." I said, "No shit. Tell me something I don't know." He laughed.

When we first met in 1971, Tom was twenty-seven, I was thirty. I was 6'1", 200 pounds, Tom was 6'2", 220 pounds, both of us athletes, pitchers, Bonus Babies. In 1965, Tom had signed at twenty-one with the Mets for a $50,000 bonus. In 1959, I had signed at eighteen with the then Milwaukee Braves for a $50,000 bonus. We were both hard-throwing right-handed pitchers destined for greatness because of our explosive fastballs. I threw harder than Tom, of course, but he will never admit to that. He had better control of his fastball than I did mine. At least I will admit to that. His career lasted longer than mine, too. Twenty years in the major leagues. I have to admit to that. It's right there in the record books.

During those twenty years, Tom Seaver started 647 games out of 656 he pitched in. He won 311 of them (eighteenth best of all time), recorded 3,640 strikeouts (sixth best), 61 shutouts (seventh best), and a lifetime earned run average of 2.86 (third best since World War II). He was one of only two major league pitchers ever to record over 300 wins, 3,000 strikeouts, and an ERA under 3.00. The other was a Hall of Famer, Walter Johnson, to whom Tom has been compared.

For such achievements Tom was voted the Rookie of the Year (1967), received three Cy Young Awards (1969, 1973, 1975), and was selected to twelve All-Star teams. In his first year on the Hall of Fame ballot, 1992, he was voted into the Hall with the highest percentage of votes, 98.84%, ever recorded at the time. Five of 450 Hall of Fame voters did not vote for him. Three omitted Seaver's name as a protest for Pete Rose's exclusion from Hall of Fame voting because of his gambling exploits. Seaver had been Rose's teammate and friend with the Reds in the '80s. A fourth voter was recovering from surgery, and he claimed he hadn't seen Seaver's name on the ballot. The fifth voter refused to vote for Seaver because, he said, he'd never vote for any candidate in his first year of eligibility. The question arises: Who were these guys, the Five Stooges? I looked for their names online but couldn't find them. Hall of Fame voters are given anonymity to protect them from their stupidity.

Tom Seaver had some great seasons, but many pitchers of lesser caliber had greater individual seasons. Denny McLain won 31 games in 1968, the last pitcher to win 30 or more games in a season. Bob Welch went 27–6 in 1990; Sandy Koufax went 25–5, 19–5, 26–8, and 27–9 between 1963 and 1966; Steve Carlton went 27–10 in 1972; Juan Marichal, 25–8 in 1963 and 26–9 in 1966; Ron Guidry, 25–3 in 1978; Pedro Martinez, 23–4 in 1999; and Randy Johnson went 24–5 in 2002.

Jim Palmer of the Orioles had the greatest run of 20-win seasons in modern baseball history. Between 1970 and 1978, Palmer won 20 or more games in seven of eight years. Yet he didn't win 300 or more games in his career. Nor did Marichal, Welch, Koufax, Guidry, Martinez, or McLain. Which may be why Hall of Famers like Marichal and Palmer, along with Bob Gibson—among other great pitchers—called Tom Seaver the greatest pitcher of their generation. Hank Aaron claimed Seaver was the toughest pitcher he ever faced.

Yet Tom Seaver won barely 20 games in a season four times, and 25 games once. His greatness was not predicated on any one season but on a twenty-year career of sustained excellence that was diminished only slightly in his forties. With the White Sox at forty and forty-one years old, Seaver won 15 and then 16 games. His greatness lies in his dogged consistency over a twenty-year career. He was among the National League's top ten pitchers in the following categories: Fewest Hits Per Season, 15 years; Most Strikeouts, Most Complete Games, Most Wins, 13 years; Lowest ERA and Most Innings Pitched, 12 seasons; Most Shutouts, 10 years; and in 10 seasons he never finished lower than eighth in Cy Young Award voting.

Some pitchers are pit bulls for a batter, an inning, a stretch of innings, a game, even a season. Tom Seaver was a pit bull on every pitch, every batter, every out, every inning, every game, every season for twenty years until he retired at forty-two. The depth of his concentration was unparalleled in the game of baseball.

Baseball players' lives are the most boring of all athletes. Their season is at least nine months long, counting spring training. Thirty-plus games during spring training, 162 games during the season, over 80 of them on the road. Road trips can be as long as fourteen days at a time. Three plane flights a week. Two hotel rooms. Room service and CNN on TV. Ten hours a day at the ballpark for a three-hour game. Tedious hours in the clubhouse playing cards, signing boxes of baseballs for strangers, watching ESPN, arguing over each other's music of choice—rap, country, whatever—all the while trying to avoid sportswriters' prying questions.

They take the field three hours before game time. Calisthenics, wind sprints, long tossing, bullpen throwing, the batting cage, an hour shagging fly balls in the outfield during batting practice. Then back to the clubhouse to change sweaty shirts, grab a snack of cold cuts and processed cheese from the lunch table. More dead time.

Finally, after six hours at the stadium, the game begins.

Position players play six games a week; starting pitchers pitch two games every ten days. When they are not pitching, starters sit in the dugout, watch the game, eat sunflower seeds, wander into the clubhouse for a coffee, call their wives, and then go back to the bench. The game is over close to midnight. Too late to get a decent meal at a nice restaurant, so they pick up something from Hardee's or KFC and take it back to their hotel room, or, if they're lucky, they find an Applebee's still open.

Baseball players' lives are filled with tedium, starting pitchers' lives more so. Which is why players say, "I play the game for nothing and get paid for the travel and the dead time." It is also why, for pitchers, it is almost impossible to maintain their concentration every game they pitch. The tedium is distracting, softens resolve, and clouds concentration, which proves unsustainable for every game. Unless you're Tom Seaver. His concentration never faltered because he loved his job, all of it. The pitching obviously, but even the dead time, too. He always found something to amuse, delight, instruct, or occupy him. There is an apocryphal story about a minor league catcher who caught the first game of a doubleheader under a hot Georgia August sun. When his manager told him he was catching the second game, too, the catcher complained. The manager waited until his catcher stopped pissing and moaning, then said, "If y'all didn'ta wanna work, son, ya shouldn'ta signed on." Tom Seaver took great pride in "signing on," but even more pride in wanting "ta work."

Still, I threw harder than Tom during my professional career. A trivial accomplishment in an inconsequential career, I know. But still, it was mine. I lasted three years in the low minor leagues of Class D teams. The McCook Braves of the Nebraska State League, the Quad Cities, Iowa, Braves of the Midwest League, the Palatka Azaleas of the Florida State League. I recorded some impressive statistics in those three low minor league seasons that were superior to Tom's statistics in a twenty-year major league career. In his career, Tom averaged 6.8 strikeouts per game, 7.5 hits per game, and recorded a career 2.86 ERA. In my career, I averaged almost 9 strikeouts per game and gave up only 7.2 hits per nine innings. My best seasons were at McCook, where I averaged 9 strikeouts a game and gave up only 6.6 hits per game, and at Quad Cities, where

I averaged 9.5 strikeouts per game and allowed 7 hits per game. My very best season, although a brief one, was in the Northeast League in 1996, when I was fifty-six. I pitched one inning for the Class AA Waterbury, Connecticut, Spirit and allowed no hits, walked one batter, struck out one, and had an ERA of 0.00. After that inning, I retired on my laurel, singular. Still, that inning did not do much for my career ERA of 4.98, or my meager 12 wins and 22 losses in 47 starts over three years and one inning. Like Tom, however, I often finished what I started. I had 13 complete games out of those 47 starts, a 28% completion percentage. Tom completed 231 games out of 647 starts, a completion percentage of 36%.

I admit my three-plus-year accomplishments, in contrast to Tom's twenty years of major league success, are not much to brag about. After all, my few successes, and many failures, were in the low minor leagues. This was brought home to me the year I turned fifty. An organization for retired minor league players sent me a letter, a pin, like a military medal, more a Purple Heart than a Bronze Star, and a red-white-and-blue baseball cap proudly identifying me as a minor league alumnus in their organization. Which was akin to memorializing my status, for all the world to see, as a professional baseball failure. Nobody plays professional baseball to be immortalized as a minor leaguer. That's like the unrepentant Confederate apologists in my little South Carolina town. They proudly wear Confederate flag T-shirts to remind themselves, and others, that they are the greatest losers in American history. You immortalize the winners, not the losers. You play minor league baseball for only one reason: to make it to the major leagues. Anything less is a failure that should haunt you. Which is why I always wear my minor league alumnus hat, to remind myself of that failure.

Still (I can't stop myself, it seems), I believe my 13 complete games were no small accomplishment in those days before pitch counts and an endless string of relief pitchers waiting in the wings. I pitched until

I couldn't get anybody out. Often, I threw over 130 pitches in a game before I was relieved with runners on base, and sometimes as many as 150 pitches in a game I completed. In the low minors, pitchers throw more pitches per batter than major league pitchers do for a number of reasons. Minor leaguers like myself, struggling with their control, threw a lot of pitches called balls by young umpires struggling like us. And a lot of strikes, too, that batters swung through without making contact. And when they did make contact, it was often a foul ball. I was always throwing 6, 7, 8, 10 pitches, or more, per batter before I got him out, or walked him, or, more rarely, he got a hit off me. My career seemed to consist of an endless series of 10-pitch 3–2 counts. We used to say in the minors in those days, it was easier to pitch in the major leagues because major league batters made quicker contact. That first-pitch fastball up and in to a minor league batter resulted in a missed swing or a foul ball. In the majors that first fastball was just as likely to be popped up to the third baseman. One pitch, one out. Today a major league pitcher's complete game is a sprint that often requires only 100 pitches or less. In the late '50s, a low minor league pitcher's complete game was often a marathon of over 130 pitches.

My failure can be traced to my greatest deficiency as a pitcher. Often on the mound, I released my fastball blissfully unaware where the ball was going once it left my hand. In the dirt, over the batter's head, straight down the middle of the plate. Tom walked a little over 2.5 batters a game; I walked almost 9 batters a game.

I remember one game in Quad Cities, in which I struck out twelve of my first fifteen batters without giving up a hit or a walk. I threw as in dream, effortless, my beautiful motion delivering fastballs that approached the batter as a white speck, as light as air, invisible, unhittable. My overhand curveball was magic. My first two managers called it "the Unfair One." It approached the plate in a meandering parabola until it appeared before the batter's lusting eyes, waist high, as big as a grapefruit. When the batter began his swing, the ball vanished. *Poof!*

It reappeared a split-second later in my catcher's glove inches off the dirt. Strike three!

In the sixth inning, I walked the first six batters I faced. The hometown fans were screaming now, "TAKE THE BUM OUT!" My teammates in the field tried to encourage me after the first few walks. "Just take a breath, Pat. Relax. You can do it." After the fourth walk they got embarrassed for me. The fans screaming, the opposing players laughing in the dugout, calling out, "Meat ain't done yet, turn him over." My teammates landscaped the infield dirt with their spikes, their eyes averted from this train wreck they could do nothing to stop. The umpires called time, bent over the plate, their asses facing me, and brushed dirt off the plate to help me see it. I shouted at them, "I can *see* the fucking thing! I just can't throw the ball over it!" Finally, after the fifth walk, my teammates got angry, too. "Throw the fucking ball over the plate!" My failure united everyone against me—my opponents, the fans, my own teammates—except for the umpires, who pitied me. They were young kids, like me, maybe a few years older. They knew what it felt like to be booed by everyone in the park when they blew a call. They despaired that I'd ever throw a pitch remotely close to the plate so they could compassionately call it a strike.

I began to fidget on the mound after each pitch, take more and more time between pitches, until finally I turned my back on the screaming fans and my laughing opponents. I stared at the centerfield flagpole. I was scared now. Frozen. Clueless. Imagine, a pitcher afraid to pitch the ball. Then, mercifully, I saw my old-timey manager, Travis Jackson, hobbling out to the mound on his spindly bowed legs. He put out his withered hand for the ball. I exhaled a great breath and surrendered it to him. He put his hand on my shoulder and said, "That's all right, son. You'll figure it out." But I never did.

I fled the mound to boos, hisses, epithets, laughter. My teammates in the dugout looked away from me. What could they say? I sat at the end of the bench, hunched over, my elbows on my knees, with a towel over my face so they couldn't see my tears.

My relief pitcher gave up a double to clear the bases. That game ended for me after five innings: 6 walks, 6 earned runs, 12 strikeouts, no hits, and another loss. The story of my career, as even Susie so rightly knew, twenty years later, without ever having seen me throw a pitch…unless you count that shot glass I fired into the darkness beside the railroad tracks. "No wonder you never made the Bigs." Oh, how cruel women can be!

By the spring of my fourth season, I was gone, back home to Connecticut. At twenty-one, a laborer for a Lithuanian mason. I was mixing mortar and lime in a tub in the cool mornings beside a new colonial house. I was alone before the mason arrived. I raked a hoe through the dried mixture that billowed up into my face, clogging my nose, burning my throat. Then I poured in water, little by little, raking the hoe through the mix until it turned into gray mud. It was back-breaking work, my body covered in cold sweat, but I made a game of it in my mind, making believe with each slash of the hoe I was throwing a fastball again. Then I carried the mud up a scaffold in two heavy paint cans with wire handles that bruised my palms. I dumped it into a tub at the top of the scaffold on the third floor of the house's unfinished chimney. When the tub was filled with mud, I began lugging bricks up the rickety scaffold that swayed in the wind. The Lithuanian mason was a dour, silent man who wouldn't let me use a metal brick carrier. He insisted I clamp five bricks between the underside of my wrist and the crook of my elbow. By the time I had stacked a neat pile of forty or so bricks beside his mud, the insides of my arms were skinned and bleeding from scraping the bricks.

When the mason arrived, he nodded, then went to the top of his scaffold, turned on a little radio to Lithuanian folk songs, and began slapping down mud, then a brick on the half-finished chimney. The scaffold swayed in the wind so much that he could only slap down mud before the scaffold leaned away from the chimney. He had to wait until the wind swayed him back so he could slap down a brick on the mud, then wait again until the wind swayed him back again so he could tap his trowel on the brick to level it. He worked steadily like this all day. When he was running low on mud or bricks, he tapped the side of his tub with his trowel as a sign for me. I hated the sound of that trowel against his tub.

I quit the mason at the end of summer and went back to college. I was married by then, with a baby. I supported my small family with odd jobs. Jerking sodas at a corner drugstore. Pumping gas on weekends. Selling Danish modern furniture at a wholesale warehouse at night. We had another baby. I graduated from college with an English degree. I got a job teaching English at an all-girls Catholic high school run by nuns. We had another baby. To supplement my $4,800-a-year teacher salary, I got a second job at a newspaper working the 6:00 p.m. to 2:00 a.m. shift for $60 a week. I wrote sports stories about high school baseball, basketball, and football games. When I was twenty-six, we had our fourth child. I picked up a third job writing a sports column for a Sunday newspaper. I was twenty-eight when our fifth child was born. Tom Seaver was already pitching for the Mets by then. After two years of modest success, 16–13 and 16–12, Tom had his first Cy Young season in 1969. He won 25 games, lost 7, and fashioned a 2.21 ERA. That was the year the Miracle Mets won the World Series, thanks to Tom, after many seasons of futility.

I began to watch Tom from afar, savoring the repetitive successes of his now golden career. I laid on the living room floor at night, my young children seated on the sofa behind me, as I watched Tom pitch on TV. With envy at first, and then grudging admiration, and finally genuine respect for his talent. I saw his mind calculating what pitch to throw each batter. I tried to think along with him: fastball up and in, slider away, slider farther away off the plate, the batter leaning over the plate now, then a fastball in on the knees, the batter jumping back from the pitch, the count 2 and 2. The batter knew Tom was going to throw another slider now on the outside corner, so he leaned over the plate again, preparing to attack Tom's slider moving off the plate and drive it down the right-field line for a double. I said out loud to the TV, "Jam him on the fists, Tom." Tom began his motion, grunted, threw. *Whoomp!* A fastball in on the batter's fists, the batter's feeble swing, strike three. My children clapped their hands with glee. "Daddy knows! Daddy knows!" I smiled. I did know. Tom and I, already buddies even if he didn't know it yet.

The more I watched Tom pitch, the more I appreciated the talent he had created through intelligence and discipline and hard work. I studied him like a student studies his professor. That graceless, plodding plowman's walk out to the mound. Shoulders hunched, head hanging, eyes on the grass, as if even that simple task deserved his utmost concentration. What was he thinking before he even reached the mound? He had the same single-focus concentration in his work as that plodding mason, but with intelligence, too. Then Tom began throwing his warm-up pitches. I could see that his motion was a conscious, painstakingly meticulous creation. Not a work of art, like my motion. But a work of craftsmanship, like that mason laying bricks. The pump, the kick, his left leg raised, his upper body curling in, the glove and ball at his chest as if to hide something, or maybe he was just gathering his concentration, and then the lunge forward, driving with his right leg, his body so low to the ground that his right knee scraped the dirt as he released the ball with brute power and a workingman's grunt. It was a compact motion for such a big man, all drawing in and then exploding out on the pitch. Nothing wasted, nothing extraneous for effect or beauty. It was just technically perfect, a tract house in Levittown designed by a pedestrian architect, every house the same, without an artist's flair or imagination.

Tom's motion was nothing like mine. I had a big, easy, effort-less-seeming motion, all style and beauty that seemed almost too graceful for a man my size. Watching me pitch was like watching a 6'1", 200-pound male ballet dancer leap and pirouette with an uncommon ease. I loved the aesthetics of my motion. I watched myself in mid-motion. I stood tall, not curled in like Tom. I had a high leg kick, my spikes above my head, my long arm stretched out behind me, windmilling back and then forward directly over my head toward the batter until I released the ball. Tom grunted the ball to the plate, all muscle and power. My big, beautiful, fluid motion carried the ball to the plate seemingly without my effort. My motion was more like Jim Palmer's of the Orioles than Tom Seaver's.

But I paid a price for that beauty. My expansive, beautifully fluid motion was susceptible to many flaws along the way because it had so many big pieces to it. If I kicked my left leg too high, it would throw off my balance on my stationary right leg. Which forced me to speed up my motion. Which caused my throwing arm to trail behind my body rather than be in sync with it. When my spikes landed in the dirt, my upper body should have been lunging toward the batter at precisely that moment when I released the ball. But when my body lunged toward the batter and my arm was still trailing behind, I lost all my body's energy on that pitch. I just flung the ball with my arm. If that pitch was a fastball, I would have flung it over the batter's head. If a curveball, it would have rolled toward the plate in a lazy arc, as big as a grapefruit to the batter's eyes.

Tom's compact, muscular, Levittown delivery precluded my flaws because it had fewer pieces to it. His smaller drawing-in motion relied less on a windmilling arm, a high leg kick, and the rhythm of an expansive motion of many moving parts than it did on the push of his powerful legs and thrust of his upper body. My work of art was almost impossible to duplicate perfectly pitch after pitch. His conscious construct of fewer and smaller moving parts made it easier for him to duplicate it pitch after pitch.

Tom's motion was earthbound, the charge of a raging bison. My motion aspired to the sun, on the feathered wings of Icarus.

Watching Tom pitch at night in those days, I had a revelation. Tom knew before I did, after it was too late for me, that it was discipline and perfection that mattered, not grace and beauty. My motion was an inspired creation without thought. A talent that was a gift. Tom's motion was a conscious construction that was hard earned. That's why I admired him so much. Not because of his talent, but because of how he had built his talent, painstakingly over years, with thought and work and dedication, and mostly with character.

In my thirties, I was no longer a struggling young writer. I was now writing for *Sports Illustrated*. Traveling a lot. Drinking too much. Too many ladies. Having problems at home. Writing books that didn't sell. Leaving home. Separating from my wife and children. And all the while I passed through those stages of an ordinary life, as most people do, I watched from a distance as Tom Seaver passed through the stages of his extraordinary life. His extraordinary career. *My* career! That was *my* life he was living. It was as if, at birth, we had been switched in the pediatrics ward by some young nurse exhausted at the end of her shift, or maybe just mooning over a young surgeon who had stopped to chat with her. And so, exhausted, or enraptured, that nurse picked up baby Tom from his crib and a few moments later accidently laid him down in the golden crib reserved for my success. Then she laid me, squalling at this miscarriage, into the crib of what should have been Tom's mundane workingman's life. It wasn't fair. I was the Golden Boy. I threw harder than Tom. I had a more beautiful motion. But there it was. Our fates sealed by a sloppy nurse.

In my forties, I was in the "process of a divorce," as they say. On the run a lot. Connecticut. Fort Lauderdale. Italy. Spain. Connecticut. Settled finally, with my second wife, Susan, in a little apartment on the Intracoastal Waterway in Fort Lauderdale. I was forty-five now, three years older than Tom. He was spending his days in the quiet seclusion of his Greenwich estate with Nancy and his two daughters. A family man. Working the crossword puzzle in the *Times* in the morning over coffee. Driving his daughters to school. Returning home to plant impatiens in clay pots. Then picking up his children from school. Going home to field business calls, offers to advertise products or give a speech, requests for interviews, and then cooking dinner. Eating dinner with his daughters and wife of twenty years, the same wife, Nancy, his only wife all these years. Tom lived the same life all the years I knew him. It was as conventional and boring as his pitching life seemed to others, twenty years of sameness, but never to him. He loved his life. Why not? He had created his family life with the same dedication and hard work he had created his career which, now, in his forties, was winding down.

Tom was preparing for his future beyond baseball, maybe a job in sports broadcasting, or maybe staying in the game as a manager or pitching coach. But not quite yet. He was still pitching, still savoring the declining yet productive years of a career by which all future careers would be judged. A Hall of Fame career. My career! Why Tom, and not me?

CHAPTER ONE

1971

Tom Seaver and I are playing games of one-on-one basketball in the Greenwich YMCA gym. It is November 1971. Two big, physical, competitive men. Me at thirty, Tom at twenty-seven. The gym is deserted except for us, banging against each other with such force that the brick walls close to the court echo with the thud of flesh against flesh. The walls are perilously close to the basket so that when we drive to the hoop and shoot, we have to raise our hands, palms out, to cushion the shock as we hit the wall.

● ● ●

I was a *Sports Illustrated* writer then, but I had been following Tom's career for years, ever since I was a teacher at that girls parochial high school in the late '60s. I saw him go from a promising young pitcher to a superstar in 1969 at the age of twenty-four.

Tom won 25 games in '69, the most of any major league pitcher that year. He lost 7 games. His earned run average was 2.21 over 273 innings in which he gave up only 202 hits, while striking out 208 batters. He completed 18 of the 35 games he started, five of them shutouts, one of them a perfect game until a lone single spoiled it in the ninth inning. He called that game the biggest disappointment in his life. Which is something only a naive youth would say who saw his life primarily in terms of professional goals he expected to surpass year after year. 1969 was that kind of season for Tom, a season of monumental successes he expected of himself, but, for others, was expected only of seasoned superstars, not baby-faced twenty-four-year-olds.

That year he led the previously hapless Mets to the first World Series Championship in the team's history. He was named the Cy Young Award winner as the best pitcher in the National League and almost was picked the league's Most Valuable Player, an unheard-of honor for a pitcher, losing out on that award by a few votes to Giants slugger Willie McCovey. One of his teammates, Ron Swoboda, said there was a "golden glow about him," and the esteemed *New Yorker* baseball writer, Roger Angell, described Tom Seaver as a man of "Galahad-like virtues."

Tom agreed. He did see himself then as heroic, even beyond baseball. Heroic enough to campaign for an end to the Vietnam War. He described himself as a "Mets Fan for Peace." To pursue that aim, Tom said it would probably be necessary for him, after the season was over, to go and "have a talk with Ted Kennedy" about how best to withdraw our troops from Vietnam.

That winter, after Tom's Cy Young Award and the Mets' World Series Championship, he and Nancy became the toast of the biggest city in the world. Everybody wanted a piece of them. Personal appearances. Magazine interviews. Paid advertisements for the usual products. They lived in New York City then and they could not hide, did not seem to want to hide. "Tom Terrific" and his stunning California-blonde wife.

Tom and Nancy's fling at being public personalities was predicated on his pitching, of course, but also on the media's defining them as "the Perfect All-American Couple." They didn't seem Californian, vapid and shallow. There was about them a kind of midwestern wholesomeness, an adult naïveté in contrast to the neurotic, intellectual cynicism of New Yorkers. Their simplicity was refreshing to New Yorkers. It was a respite from their cynicism, as innocence often is for cynics, but not for long. One writer called Tom a "Huck Finn of a pitcher," which is interesting. Huck was always a more devious youth than his friend, the innocent Tom Sawyer.

The Seavers appeared frequently on TV talk shows as the loving young couple. Tom said that his wife and baseball were the two most important things in his life. They were rumored to be about to host their own TV talk show, *The Tom and Nancy Seaver Hour*. They were the subjects of numerous flattering magazine articles. Were willing, it seemed, to advertise any and everything, including themselves, for a price. They offered themselves to advertisers in a New York newspaper ad in which they presented themselves as a couple as "American as Apple Pie." Tom was America's most famous athlete, and Nancy was Tom's lovely wife, "a young Mrs. America with sales appeal."

Within a year their publicity blitz began to backfire for a number of reasons. It began with a post-World Series trip to Las Vegas for Tom and some of his teammates. The players were advised not to bring their wives along, as the city still had its "Sin City, What Happens in Vegas, Stays in Vegas" reputation. The players obliged, except for Tom. He brought Nancy. The other players felt foolish, conspicuous as famous married men in Vegas without their wives, while one of their number, the most famous of them all, was always seen with his wife in the casinos.

Actually, Tom's teammates were conflicted about his often-avowed faithfulness to his wife. On the one hand, they would like to have emulated it. On the other hand, they saw it as Tom's affront to their unfaithfulness to their wives. As if that was his intent. But such posturing as the faithful husband assumed a deviousness Tom never had. The players were reading into Tom's motives what was in their minds, not his. If Tom had a flaw, and he had many, it was blunt honesty. Even if he ever did cheat on Nancy, he could never then posture as the faithful husband. In his mind that would be two deceits, the second maybe worse even than the first in his eyes.

In Vegas, the players glad-handed patrons in casinos and appeared on stage with comedians and sang songs, for which they were paid equally and handsomely. Tom, however, felt, as the most famous player on the Mets, who had contributed the most to their getting to the World Series, that he should be paid more than his teammates. Which did not sit well with them. Even if Tom was right.

A few of Tom's teammates felt that not only in Vegas, but in general, Nancy was always hogging the spotlight from their own wives. She was the beautiful, blonde wife the camera lingered on at Shea Stadium in between innings. The beautiful wife TV broadcasters turned to for interviews, about herself, and her famous husband, which brought her her own fame. On TV shows as a couple, Tom bragged about how beautiful his wife was. Nancy bragged that she was "not a losing pitcher's wife." Nancy more than held her own on such shows, with Tom as her wingman, but when she ventured off on her own for a prominent women's magazine profile of the famous pitcher's wife, it was a disaster.

Nancy went to lunch at an exclusive "ladies who lunch" restaurant in the city with a woman writer. Nancy spent that lunch being cute. When her dessert arrived, the writer described Nancy talking to it ("Hello, dessert!"). When its remnants were removed by the waiter, Nancy bid her half-eaten dessert a sad farewell ("Goodbye, dessert!") with a little flutter of her fingers. When that article appeared, it turned Nancy's growing image as "America's Sweetheart," the Meg Ryan of *Sleepless in Seattle*, on its head. It fostered a new image of Nancy more akin to the image of Meg Ryan of too much bad plastic surgery and *In the Cut*. A calculating, dim-witted California blonde.

Tom didn't help his wife redeem her image in that profile when he reluctantly let that writer interview him. He was curt, condescending, arrogant. "I took journalism courses in college," he told her. "I know what most reporters are up to."

By the beginning of the 1970 season, the tone of the stories about Tom and Nancy had begun to change. Roger Angell had written earlier that there was "an unpleasantly planned aspect to [Tom's] golden image." But Angell's perceptions could be dismissed as an aberration, since he viewed the game and its players from a great distance, through the eyes of a fan. Angell rarely talked to Tom, and never in depth, unlike the newspaper beat writers, who talked to Tom daily. But now even sportswriters, who did spend a lot of time talking to Tom, became more critical of every word out of his mouth.

Tom never minded talking to sportswriters after one of his many triumphs before 1970. He would lecture them, somewhat pedantically, on the finer points of his pitching mastery, or, on rare occasions, explain to them how even his flawed performances taught him "a lesson in maturity" that led to "a moment of personal growth." Tom may have been the only pitcher in baseball who turned a poorly pitched game into a positive experience that made him a better pitcher. This pop psychobabble played well with the sportswriters—Tom Seaver, the thinking man's pitcher.

In 1970, Tom had, for him, a mediocre year. He won 18 games and lost 12, but won only one of his last ten starts. The New York sportswriters began to take pleasure in the mediocrity of the man they had labeled "Tom Terrific." "Tom Terrific" wasn't so terrific after all. He was like them, mortal, no longer a god. For the first time in his four years with the Mets, Tom heard a smattering of boos when he took the mound, and louder boos when he left it prematurely. Tom now went out of his way to avoid fans.

Toward the end of the 1970 season, Tom stopped explaining himself to writers. No more didactic dissertations on his pitching. No more in-depth interviews. He felt that, no matter how he explained himself, they'd twist his words to make him look foolish. Maybe they wanted to make him look foolish? So, no more philosophizing now. Just the facts, ma'am. Writer: "Why'd that two-twenty hitter beat you with a home run, Tom?" Tom: A dismissive look. And then, "Because I hung a curveball."

Writers trotted out new words to describe Tom Seaver. Money-hungry, plastic, selfish, phony, calculating, closed.

Even a few teammates were losing patience with Tom. Ron Swoboda went on record saying he found it distasteful the way Tom "marketed" Nancy to make money. Swoboda called Tom "self-centered," with no "feeling for people." Tom fired back with unconcealed sarcasm that Swoboda's analysis of Tom Seaver's nature was the psychology of "one of the greatest self-analysts of our time."

Tom was no dummy. After the 1970 season, he and Nancy, abruptly and surreptitiously, abandoned their New York City apartment and their public visibility for the seclusion and serenity of a country farmhouse in Connecticut. There, Tom deliberately began to cultivate, along with the flowers in his garden, a studied "dullness" that freed him from public scrutiny. He devoted his days to gardening, working the crossword puzzle in the *New York Times*, converting mailboxes into flowerpots for his daughter. He became a boring interview subject who talked only about his pitching. Writers drifted away. Seaver wasn't that interesting after all. He was just another not-very-bright California jock. Magazine spreads about the "All-American Couple" vanished. So did *The Tom and Nancy Seaver Hour* TV show. Talk-show hosts no longer invited them to be guests to discuss their perfect life. Advertisers no longer made offers. Word spread. Tom and Nancy were as dull as dishwater, dumb as dirt, *uninteresting*: the kiss of death in Manhattan. "That pleased me just fine," Tom told me once.

Tom and Nancy's newly cultivated dullness freed them both. She could be herself, a not unintelligent but somewhat conventional young woman, unburdened by others' misperceptions because of her beauty. She was content in her life as a wife and mother, without the need to be a public spectacle. Tom's mind was now uncluttered with extraneous worries, his energies untapped, his concentration intense again for that which he called "the most important thing I do in my life. Pitch."

I watched all this from afar while I was writing stories for *SI* from 1969 to 1971, most of them profiles of pitchers. I came to believe that, beneath Tom's clunky, rote introspection, he was not only an exceptional pitcher but an exceptional man, too. I was intrigued. And not a little jealous.

So I called him.

I had been badgering my *Sports Illustrated* editor, Ray Cave, to let me write a profile of Tom for two years. He played me off each time. Finally, I challenged him.

"Give me a reason," I said.

"He's boring."

"Not to me."

"He's been done."

"Not by me he hasn't."

Ray smiled. "Well then, if you think you can get something out of him, go ahead and tell me what you see." Ray was the articles editor at *SI*, and my rabbi there. He had discovered my writing in a slush pile of newspaper columns I had sent him. Whenever he gave me an assignment, he always said the same thing: "Go there and tell me what you see." He never gave me direction or a list of points he wanted me to pursue, as other editors after him would. Just, "Go there and tell me what you see." The first time he said this I asked him what he meant. He said, "You have a unique way of seeing things. You see things always three degrees off center." I was crushed. As a beginning writer, I thought it was my job to see things the same way other writers did.

So in the fall of '71, I called the Mets' media liaison and asked him to set up an interview for me with Tom Seaver. The media guy said he was busy. "Here," he said, "this is his home number. You can call him yourself."

So I called Tom. He answered the phone. I introduced myself. Before I could tell him I was an *SI* writer and I wanted to write a story about him, he said, "I know who you are. I read your pitchers' stories." I waited for him to compliment me on them, or maybe criticize them. Nothing. My introduction to Tom Seaver. A man of few words, for whom everything was in his silences. His silence *was* the compliment.

I told Tom I had been a pitcher, too, in the Braves organization. He said, "I know that." I asked him if I could interview him for an *SI* profile. He said, "Why? I'm boring."

I said, "Not to me." Silence.

Then he said, "When do you want to do it?"

"Whenever it's convenient."

"Well then, let's get it done. I'm going to the Greenwich YMCA to shoot some hoops in an hour. Do you play basketball?"

"Yeah. I had a few college basketball scholarship offers out of high school."

He said, "Really?" in that high-pitched voice of his I would learn underlined his sarcasm. "Scholarships, huh? Maybe you're too good for me. If you go easy on me, I'll try to give you a good game." He laughed. "Pick me up in an hour. We'll play a little one-on-one…just for fun." Then he laughed again and hung up. It was a scary laugh.

⬟　⬟　⬟

Tom has the ball close to the hoop. He gives me a head fake. I go up. As I come down, he goes up. His shoulder clips me on the jaw. I see stars. The ball goes in the basket. I rotate my jaw to see if it's broken.

"You all right?" Tom says, without interest, as he takes the ball out to half-court.

"Why not?" I say, and smile at him.

We have been playing like this for hours. We are both drenched with sweat. Our faces red and swollen from exhaustion and the fierceness of our competition. Tom is only an adequate basketball player. Graceless, clumsy, which is to his advantage. It gives him an excuse for his blatant fouls. But he has strong hands, like a vice. Once he gets close to the hoop he is unstoppable. His basic move is to back in to the basket, left-right-left-right, until he is close enough to throw in his short jump shot. Even with me hanging on his arms he is still strong enough to put the ball in the hoop.

I am a much better shooter than Tom. I have a greater variety of shots and a velvet touch. Tom has the touch of a blacksmith, the ball clanking off the rim when he misses. Tom gets furious when I dribble the ball nonchalantly beyond the keyhole and then suddenly go up for a thirty-foot jump shot. *Swish!* When I try to get close to the basket, he slows me down with a shoulder to my gut. But I do the same to him. Neither of us ever calls a foul. No blood, no foul. Not even when there is blood.

So Tom backs in toward the hoop, bent over double, his big ass pushing me backward. I thrust my hips against him to stop him. *Whack!* He pushes me back with ass. I push back. *Whack!* He pushes. *Whack!* Push! *Whack!* Finally, he gets close enough to the hoop for his pathetic little jump shot. He goes up. I time my jump perfectly and slap the ball back into his face. It bounces high into the air. Without wiping the blood from his nose, Tom leaps for the ball, snares it, comes down, goes up again, this time with the top of his head aimed at my jaw. Clunk. I see stars again. I go backpedaling into the brick wall. The ball hits the backboard, rattles around the rim before falling through. Tom grins. Blood trickles down his nose.

"You all right?" he says again as he walks to half-court with the ball.

"Sure. Want me to get you some Kleenex for your nose?" He glares at me over his shoulder. I smile.

We go on like this for hours. He wins a game. I win a game. He wins a game. I win a game. Finally, after too many games to count, we agree that the winner of the next game wins the day. For what? Bragging rights? The writer proves he's an athlete, too? The pitcher proves his will overcomes the writer's talent? No. We're just two jocks who hate to lose.

By this time we are both bruised and scraped, our T-shirts speckled with dried blood, our knees and elbows raw and skinned. There is a pulsating welt on the side of my head. It feels like something is growing out of it, an alien being from a horror movie. Tom's nose is a swollen, flaming pink, like a pig's. The dried blood caked on his upper lip looks like Hitler's mustache.

The last game is tied. The next basket wins. Tom has the ball at the top of the key. He is dribbling around to catch his breath. I am panting like a rabid dog, foaming at the mouth. My body aches in places I never knew existed. I am crouched over, waiting for Tom to back into the hoop, his only move—dumb, brute force. Not this time, Big Guy. I plant my feet, spread wide like a defensive lineman in football about to sack the quarterback. Hurt him, too. Make him think twice the next time.

But he surprises me. He takes a dribble and a long stride, then drives straight to the hoop. He is past me before I recover and follow him. Just as he is about to go up for a layup, I am ready to push him in the back with both hands. Let's see if the prick calls a foul this time. I want to hear him whine. Then I see the wall in front of him. In my mind's eye I see him slamming into that brick wall, hear the sickening crack of his arm breaking against the bricks…Tom Seaver's arm! Jesus, God! I drop my hands as he lays the ball in the basket.

It is raining outside the Greenwich gym. We get in my car and drive back to Tom's farmhouse. My car is an old Corvette with a T-top roof that rattles and leaks. It is painted gold. When Tom saw my gold Corvette when I picked him up at his house, he laughed out loud. "Nice color," he said.

Now we are driving back to his house for lunch. He looks around the ragged interior of my 'Vette and says, "Why didn't you buy a Porsche?"

"I have a Porsche," I said. "And a Ferrari, too. This is just my knock-around car when I don't have to impress anyone."

He shook his head. "Is that a compliment or an insult?"

"Both."

"Seriously, though. Why didn't you get a Porsche?"

I look across at him. "Because I'm not Tom Seaver, that's why."

He nods. "That's a fact." Rain is seeping through the T-top roof that rattles. Tom looks up. Water drips on his forehead. He blinks, wipes off the water with the back of his hand. He says, "It leaks."

"No shit." I am hunched forward over the steering wheel, wiping off the fogged window with my bare hand so I can see the traffic.

"Put on the defroster," Tom says. I glare at him. He says, "That, too?" He laughs in that high-pitched, girlish way of his that always would infuriate me.

"You know, I let you win that last game," I say.

"You did, huh?" He raises his eyebrows.

"Yeah, if you were anyone else, I would have pushed you into the fucking wall."

He looks over at me, his eyebrows still raised, a faint smile on his lips. "Bullshit, Jordan! I don't know much about you, but I know one thing. You never let anyone win at anything in your life."

"Usually you'd be right. But I let *you* win today. I mean, you're Tom Fucking Seaver, a big fucking star. I coulda broke your arm." He doesn't answer. Finally, I say, "You know what else?"

"What?"

"I threw harder than you."

"In your fucking dreams."

"No, I did, Tom. I just didn't know where it was going." We both laugh.

Tom's right. I do have to win every game. I have to perfect everything. It's exhausting. At the end of the day I have nothing left.

"What about you?" I say. "You're the same."

Serious now, he says, "About pitching, yes. But not everything. I don't waste my energy on unimportant things. Or things I don't understand."

It is rainy and cold when we reach the stony dirt road that leads to his modest farmhouse. My 'Vette rattles and shakes over the rutted road. When I hit a high spot in the road the undercarriage scrapes against the dirt. I look over at Tom. He shrugs and says, "I'm not saying a word."

We go inside and Tom shows me around. The house is immaculate, sparingly furnished with wooden antiques. He leads me downstairs to the cellar. Dirt floor, stone walls. One wall is layered with fireplace flues laid end to end. Twenty flues in each row, twenty rows in all. It looks like a huge honeycomb for giant mutant bees. However, a few of the flues have wine bottles in them, lying on their sides.

"I built it myself," he says.

"I wouldn't have the patience," I say.

"I know. It was repetitious work. But I never got bored. Every flue I laid out was a complete-game victory. Every row was a twenty-win season." He waves the back of his hand at the flues. "Twenty years of twenty-win seasons. I loved it. When I finished I began to panel around it. When I came to a water pipe that stuck out of the wall, I couldn't figure out how to panel around it. It was beyond my comprehension."

"Now that would have driven me nuts until I figured it out."

Tom nods. "I almost lost interest in it. Eventually I did panel it all. But it's far from perfect. I can live with the imperfections. I don't have the stamina and mental concentration to do everything with the same intensity I pitch." He smiles at me. "Not like you. You've got to perfect everything, I bet. You can't let anything go."

"Yeah. It's exhausting being me."

"I'll bet you're one of those guys who's got to find out about himself every morning. You're always digging deeper than things are. Life isn't that heavy for me. I don't have to figure myself out. Win every basketball game. My competitiveness is like an energy source. It has limits. So I save it for pitching. If I use it up on too many things, I won't have enough left for pitching." He laughs. "I really don't know, though. I never think about such things."

"Why do you pitch?"

"I don't think about why. Philosophically, that is. What does it mean? It excites me. That's enough."

Tom is not comfortable with abstractions. He distrusts them. He has a reporter's intelligence. His mind is sensitive to experiences, to facts. How to do something, not why. But he's an intelligent man, too quick to shortchange himself. His reach never exceeds his grasp. He is disinclined to intuit beyond experience. Things must happen to him first before he can figure them out. I care first about the why, not the how. I have to intuit everything before it happens so I can defend against the bad stuff. My reach always exceeds my grasp, which is sometimes rewarding, sometimes frustrating.

In the minor leagues, my pitching coach, a prissy man with glasses like an accountant, tried to change my pitching motion to help me throw strikes. "Drop your shoulder down a bit," he said. "Why?" I said. "Just do it," he said. "But why?" I said. That night he sent in his scouting report to the Braves' front office. He wrote that Jordan was uncoachable. Why?

Standing on the pitcher's mound, Tom has ocular block. He sees only the batter through a narrow tunnel, as if through a sniper's rifle scope.

On the mound I used to see the batter through fractured light darting everywhere. I try to concentrate on the batter. I begin my motion, pump, raise my leg, am distracted by a farmer in bib overalls sitting in the stands, a towheaded boy with a baseball glove waiting for a foul ball, a pretty girl in a summer dress walking up the aisle, and overhead, a blinding sun. My concentration has always been diffused. I see it all, in an instant. A curse for an athlete, but a blessing for a writer.

When I first met Tom I was thirty, but I looked forty. Dark skin, weather-beaten face, curly black hair, bushy eyebrows. Dark eyes. Unsmiling. A little bit threatening. Scowling. When I was sixteen, a junior at a Jesuit prep school, I looked thirty. One of the old Jesuits used to pull me out of class every other day. A thin, frail man smelling of body odor beneath his black cassock. With a quivering hand, he pressed a five-dollar bill into my palm. "Get me a fifth of Seagram's, Mr. Jordan," he would say. In those days, the mid-'50s, priests could not wear laymen's clothes and so they were easily identifiable as priests around our small town. So I went to the liquor store and bought a fifth of Seagram's for that poor priest every other day. The liquor store owner said to me once, "You're awful young to have a drinking problem, son." The drinking age in Connecticut was twenty-one, but I was never carded. If it was Tom, he would have been carded until he turned thirty.

At twenty-seven, he looked like a boy, not a man. A little soft. Amiable. Smiling. A smooth, unlined face. Unthreatening. A Norman Rockwell face. Sandy-colored hair neatly parted on one side. A boy's innocent pale-brown eyes. But still a handsome face. The boring handsomeness of Pat Boone and Tab Hunter in the '50s. It's tempting to look at Tom, even today, in his seventies, and see a face without character. But that would be a mistake. It's a deceptive face, without characteristics, but with more character than I ever had when I first met him. I may have looked older, more mature, a man, but I was more a hyperactive boy (my parents called me "too sensitive") when

I first met Tom. He had been a man in control of himself many years before I was.

Tom and I are sitting at an old farm table in his kitchen. Tom is preparing a late lunch for us both. A New York strip sirloin for him and a filet mignon the size of a catcher's mitt for me. He puts the steaks under the broiler and goes back to our salad. He has tomatoes, onions, celery stalks, and cucumbers lined up on a cutting board. He begins to slice the cucumbers into identically thin rounds with the machine-gun rapidity of a professional chef.

Tom looks up from his slicing, smiles, and says, "I love this. The methodicalness of it. Is that a word?"

"If it isn't, it should be."

"I have to defer to you on some things. Maybe 'monotony' is a better word. Whatever. It relaxes me." It isn't until years later, in my forties, that I learn to appreciate the pleasure of preparing and cooking food to please others.

When the steaks are done, he puts them on our plates.

After we eat our lunch, we go into the living room to drink our beers. Slider, his small chocolate-colored dog, trots after us. I sit on a worn sofa while Tom lights a fire in his old stone fireplace. He puts bits of torn-up newspaper under pieces of kindling.

"Tom, the newspaper! That's a sacrilege. Some poor bastard wrote those stories and you're gonna incinerate them."

"Watch," he says with glee. He lights a long wooden match in his right hand, then transfers it to his left hand and lights the paper in the fireplace. When the kindling catches fire Tom picks up a few pieces of split wood, holds them under his right arm, then transfers one after another to his left hand before he puts them on top of the burning kindling. He notices me watching him.

Then he sits down in a big easy chair and watches his handiwork flame up and spread warmth through the cold farmhouse living room.

Slider lies down beside him. Tom absentmindedly reaches down his left hand to pet Slider behind his ears. Tom knows what I'm thinking before I put it into a question.

"It's not only throwing wood into a fire with my left hand," he says. "I pet dogs only with my left hand, too."

"Even Slider?"

"Especially Slider. He's a reminder when I pet a strange dog. I used to have to remind myself about these things, but now they're force of habit. Like dieting on January 2 of every year. No more chocolate chip cookies. No more beer and fried eggs for breakfast. Cottage cheese and sliced apples now." He looks at me and says, "You know, I actually like that cottage cheese now. I learned to like it because of what it meant. Less weight to lose in spring training. Less time it took for me to get into midseason shape before spring training broke."

But it is only November. He gets himself another beer. Relaxes. Tries to, anyway. Something is bothering him. We sit in silence for a while. Then he says, "I'm having contract problems with the Mets. I hate it. Squabbling with Scheffing [Bob Scheffing, the Mets' general manager] over money." The Mets have offered him $100,000 less than Tom thinks he's worth. It is the principle as much as it is the money to Tom. I know how he feels. One of the first words I learned in Italian from my parents, when I was ten, was *rispetto*. When someone gives you *rispetto*, it's the highest form of compliment. It means they value greatly what you are. And when they don't give you *rispetto*, it's the basest insult a person can be given. It's a matter of personal pride.

Tom is a prideful man. Not about everything, but about some things. His wife and his pitching. Which is ironic to me. This WASPy-looking white-bread, with blond hair and pale brown eyes, has the same kind of Italian values I was raised with. *Rispetto*. Which is why, over all the years I have known him, he always takes my bait and bristles when I tell him I threw harder than he did. I do it with such confidence and satisfaction—"I threw harder than you, Tom"—that his face turns red and he challenges me: "In your fucking dreams, Jordan." But left there, in the recesses of his mind is…doubt.

I commiserate with him. The unfairness of it all. Offering him $100,000 less than he is worth. Tom says, in his shrill voice, "How do they expect me to support my family?" Tom has two little girls. I had five children by the time I was his age now. At that time, I made $6,400 a year as a schoolteacher and sports columnist for a Sunday newspaper.

No matter how exceptional a man Tom Seaver is for a famous athlete, he still has a famous athlete's self-absorption. He floats above the complex and disagreeable facts of life for ordinary people. Their problems are not real to him. When Tom asked me why I didn't buy a Porsche instead of my ratty old 'Vette, he was serious. He would have bought a Porsche. In his world, my refusal to trade up to a Porsche was not a sign of my diminished circumstances but of my adolescent need for flash. Gold?

I wonder, if I had been driving toward the hoop for the winning basket in the Greenwich Y gym, would Tom have hesitated to push me into the brick wall?

Tom makes an effort to overcome his bad mood over his contract squabbles for my benefit. He begins to tell me a funny story about Dick Schaap, the wealthy sportswriter, and his wife. They live up the road from Tom in a big old white colonial home on an estate with an expansive front lawn.

Tom and Nancy went to dinner at the Schaaps' one night. Dinner was served by a black maid in a white uniform. Over dinner, Schaap's wife entertained them with stories of her previous love affairs. Dick just sat there silent, with a cuckold's smile. Tom and Nancy looked down at their plates. The maid entered with a huge rib roast that looked like it had been carved out of a mastodon. Everyone began to eat. An hour later everyone was stuffed. And still half of the rib roast was left. Tom and Dick sat back and lit cigars. Schaap's wife tinkled a little bell. The maid appeared. Mrs. Schaap told her to dispose of the remaining rib roast. The maid picked up the silver tray with the remnants of the roast and carried it into the kitchen. Tom and Dick were talking. The maid left the door open. Tom began to laugh at something Dick said, and then, out of the corner of an eye, through the haze of his cigar smoke, he saw the maid about to dump the rib roast into a garbage pail.

Tom shrieked like a woman, "Stop!" Everyone looked at him. The maid stared at him through the doorway. "Don't throw that away!" Then, to Mrs. Schaap, Tom said, "If you're not gonna eat that, I'll take it home." And he did.

Tom shakes his head in disbelief and says to me, "Can you imagine? That roast fed my family for a week."

I hear the screen door of the old farmhouse spring open, then snap shut. Nancy enters the living room with shopping bags from Bloomingdale's and Saks and Bergdorf Goodman dangling from both hands. Designer bags and boxes, not grocery bags.

She says, brightly, "Hello, boys."

Tom introduces me. I stand up and shake Nancy's hand. She says, "The writer." She smiles and says, "Thomas doesn't trust writers. But you know that, don't you."

"I'd heard. But he's been the perfect interview." I smile at her. "I let him win in basketball."

"He let you win, Thomas? You must have loved that. Or didn't you notice?"

"He never let me win," Tom said. "He doesn't know how to let anyone win."

"Just like you, Thomas."

Nancy is blonde, pretty, with a brilliant false smile that reveals nothing. I already know how she's been portrayed in the press. The typical cute, dim baseball star's wife. It's a portrayal she does not work to dispel. Yet she looks less cute than interestingly attractive. Prominent cheekbones that are almost Indian-like, a wide, sensuous mouth, blue eyes, and a lazy, lilting, girlishly breathless way of talking that seems vaguely Southern. Still, her hair is bleached a too-bright blonde. I remember what my older brother told me when I was a teenager. "Two things you've got to remember about 'dumb blondes,' brother," he said. "They're never blonde, and they're never dumb."

Nancy holds up her packages and says, "I've been shopping."

"Really?" Tom says. Then to me, he says, "You know, shopping is Nancy's 'very most favorite thing in the world.'" He nods, grinning. "No kidding."

Nancy, mock frowning, says, "Now, Thomas, you know that's not true. Shopping is only my 'second very most favorite thing in the world.' My 'very most favorite thing in the world' is lying in the sun for eight hours a day."

Tom, glancing at me, raises his eyebrows and says, "Do you believe it?"

"Well, boys, I think I'll just leave you to your business." She flashes her dazzling false smile. "I'll be upstairs putting away all these little things I bought with Thomas's money."

Tom and I watch her go up the stairs. When her upper body disappears above the second-floor landing, she stops. She leans down so that her face is visible to us below the landing. Still smiling, she says, "By the way, Thomas. Did Mr. Scheffing call today?"

Tom's face turns red and she is gone.

CHAPTER TWO
1972

Tom and I, Tom Sawyer and Huck Finn, are walking barefoot in the sand alongside the placid blue-green waters of the Gulf of Mexico on Madeira Beach, Florida. I am shirtless in the sun, my upper body glistening with suntan oil. I want to catch some rays for my tan. It highlights my abs. Tom is wearing a baseball cap pulled low over his forehead, an oversized gray T-shirt, and baggy Bermuda shorts. His face and arms and legs are pasty white. I ask him if he uses mayonnaise for suntan oil. He smiles and says, "And what do you use…olive oil?"

I pick up flat stones and scale them across the water. Tom is flying a kite. It's a speck high up in the cloudless sky. The sky is swarming with the flap and caw of seagulls. Big, grayish, heavy-breasted birds, they must beat their wings furiously, stomachs heaving, necks straining forward, so that for one brief moment they can level off and glide with a hard-earned, uncommon grace.

"Aren't they fascinating?" Tom says to me. "The way they work at it. I could watch them for hours. I'd love to fly like the gulls. But I can't. So I pitch. If I couldn't pitch, I'd do something else." He looks at me. "But if I could pitch and wasn't, that would bother me, a lot."

For nine months a year, Tom lives his life around the five-day span between each start. It determines what he eats, when he goes to bed, what he does or doesn't do when he's awake. He doesn't go shirtless in the Florida sun. He might get a burn, which would inhibit his throwing. When he wakes in the morning, he doesn't read the book or movie reviews in the *New York Times*. He goes directly to the box scores on the sports pages to see who got two hits off Bill Singer last night. He pets dogs and throws logs on a fire with his left hand. He diets constantly. He learned such precautions from Walt Payne, an old-time semipro player, when he was a kid.

"It made sense to me," Tom says. "Now I'm very conscious of using my right hand for anything. I learned to enjoy dieting, too. Cut out the chocolate chip cookies. I'm happiest when I pitch well, so I only do those things that make me happy. It's not money or glory that motivates me. It doesn't motivate me to be the fastest pitcher who ever lived, like some guys." He gives me a little smile.

"Yeah, I know guys like that," I say.

"I'll bet you do. They have to be the fastest, or get the most strikeouts, or have the greatest season. I just want to do the best I can, day after day, year after year, and then it'll happen."

"What will happen?"

"I'll prove I'm the best ever."

I laugh out loud. "And I thought I had a big ego."

Tom shrugs, gives me an embarrassed smile. "What can I say?"

Tom Seaver is the youngest pitcher ever to sign a $100,000-a-year contract. He's averaged almost 19 wins a season in his first four years with the Mets, whose normal finish during that span was fifth place. At twenty-seven, he has already won 75 games, more wins in those first four years than Grover Cleveland Alexander, Sandy Koufax, Warren Spahn, and Bob Gibson.

The following morning, Tom and I are standing behind the batting cage at the Mets' spring training complex in St. Petersburg, watching the team take batting practice. Tom's cheek is puffed out with chewing tobacco. I am smoking a cigar. A lazy spring training morning in March under a hot sun and a strong breeze off the Gulf. A few old men in Bermuda shorts and black knee socks are clustered together, like old crones, in the exposed bleachers. Teenage girls in small shorts are hanging out close to the field, practicing seductive smiles. Long-haired boys are lying insouciantly on the bleachers, their bony chests shirtless in the sun. Small boys wearing Mets caps and T-shirts are hustling after foul balls.

On the field the air is filled with shrill whistles, exhortations of "Attaboy, Stud," the crack of a bat against a ball, the slap of a ground ball into a glove. Sportswriters are talking to players around the field, in the dugout, scribbling in their notebooks.

Tom and I are watching Ed Kranepool hit. The Mets' left-handed-hitting first baseman. "Easy Ed." A big man, 6'4", 250 pounds, all soft flesh and no muscle. He moves in slow motion as if to conserve energy, like a three-toed sloth. Or maybe because he is bored. Or he just woke up. Or maybe somnambulism is his constant state of being. He swings. A big, slow roundhouse of a swing. The ball rises lazily into the sky. The wind carries the ball toward the center-field fence, where it dies of inertia. A pitcher, shagging balls in the outfield, camps under it and snares it ten feet from the fence.

Tom shakes his head. He spits tobacco juice through the batting screen and makes a little sound of disgust. He says, sotto voce, to me, "You know, he hit twenty balls to the warning track last year. Twenty fucking balls. Another ten feet and they would have been home runs. I know I'd find the strength *somewhere* to hit those balls another ten feet." He spits again.

"Easy Ed" swings, a lazy fly ball to right. Two pitchers jostle each other playfully until one snaps the ball out of the air ten feet from the right-field wall. Tom looks at me, his eyes wide. "Do you fucking believe it? I mean, if you don't think baseball is a big deal, don't do it. But if you do it, do it right!"

I mention Bo Belinsky, the former playboy pitcher with the California Angels, who dissipated a promising career with broads and booze. "I spent a week with him recently," I say. "He's living in a cathouse in Hollywood Hills."

"What a fool he must be to throw it all away like that," says Tom.

I say, "But he's a good guy, Tom. You'd like him."

But Tom wouldn't like Bo. He can't hide his disdain for men who don't have the character to fulfill their potential. He sees it as a weakness not in his nature. One of Tom's few flaws as a man. He can't get out of himself. He judges players by his standards, although not by his successes. He prefers to spend his time with men like Bud Harrelson and Jerry Grote, teammates who work very hard at their pedestrian talent. Overachievers, like he himself once was.

When Tom was a high school senior in Fresno, California, he was the third-best pitcher on his team. His fastball clocked in the mid-eighties. "I was small," he says, "five-nine, a hundred fifty-five pounds. I won five games and lost four that year. Jeez, I'd never been the star of any team." So he began to lift weights to put on muscle. The muscle came slowly. So he joined the Marine Corps after high school. After six months he had lost his baby fat and gained a little muscle, a lot of discipline, and an appreciation for hard work. When he left the Marine Corps Reserves in 1963, he enrolled at Fresno City College as a dental student. He fashioned an 11–2 record in his freshman year of pitching. After the season, Dodgers scout Tommy Lasorda offered Tom a $3,000 bonus to sign with the Dodgers. Tom asked for $50,000. Lasorda wished him well as a dentist.

USC coach Rod Dedeaux had watched Tom pitch a few City College games that year and expressed mild interest in giving him a scholarship. But first he suggested Tom go to Alaska to pitch for the Alaska Goldpanners of Fairbanks in a tough collegiate summer league. Almost overnight in Alaska, it seems, Tom shot up to 6'1", gained thirty pounds of muscle, and added almost 10 mph to his fastball. When he returned to California, Dedeaux gave him a scholarship. In his sophomore year, Tom won ten games and lost two at USC and was drafted number one in the 1966 winter draft by the Milwaukee Braves, signing a $50,000 bonus contract. The Braves had always been his favorite team, Hank Aaron his favorite player. Tom loved the Braves' uniforms with the tomahawk across the chest and the patch of an Indian warrior on the sleeve. The same uniform I put on that first day I signed for my $50,000 bonus contract in 1959 in Milwaukee County Stadium. I thought that uniform was a bit garish even at eighteen years old. I had always dreamed of wearing a snow-white uniform with navy pinstripes in Yankee Stadium.

Tom's Braves contract was voided by Major League Baseball because Tom's USC team had played two exhibition games in the spring, which made him ineligible for the draft. MLB wouldn't have even known about those two meaningless games, neither of which Tom had pitched in, if, it was rumored, Dedeaux hadn't informed the league. He had no intention of losing his star pitcher so soon. Now Tom couldn't play in the pros, and the NCAA wouldn't let him return to college because he was considered a pro after signing the Braves contract. Tom's father, Charles, threatened to sue Major League Baseball, and the commissioner's office relented. MLB then instituted a special draft for just one player, Tom Seaver. A lottery was held for any team that would at least match the Braves' offer, which led to Tom's signing with the New York Mets.

● ● ●

"I never had anything handed to me," Tom says. "Pitching has always been awful hard work for me. I was aware of my physical limitations at fourteen. I had to adjust. It was a burden then, but obviously it helped me."

At fourteen, pitching became for Tom a mental activity as well as a physical one. If he could do nothing yet to enhance his physical talent, he could still cultivate his understanding of his craft. He learned that hitters feed off pitchers' mistakes. So he would make none. If he couldn't throw his fastball past batters, he could at least throw it where they couldn't hit it solidly. Bases on balls were the curse of pitchers, so he refused to walk batters. "Walking hitters bothered me even then," Tom says. "It was so…free!"

Tom discovered that his control and his stuff were both directly related to his pitching motion. So he created a motion that gave him maximum use of his modest talents. It was simple, direct, controlled. The same motion pitch after pitch. If, in mid-motion, he felt a flaw in his delivery, he corrected it…in mid-motion. Even the best of pitchers can correct a flaw only after the flawed pitch. Most get trapped in their flaw, pitch after pitch, without a clue how to correct it.

Tom also learned how it felt to be shelled unmercifully in one inning and then have to walk out to the mound to start the next. "It's a terrible feeling," he said. "You want to quit. You feel it's hopeless. But you have to forget the last inning, the bad pitches, and start all over like it never happened. Some guys can't do that. They're always fighting things in the past beyond their control."

I tell Tom what my father had told me when I was a boy. "He said, 'The past is baggage, kid. It makes you miss the next train out.'" I laugh, then say, "But he never told me to where."

Tom just nods, then he says, "I learned to let my talent dictate what I was as a pitcher on any given day. I adjusted to its limits. I couldn't do more than I was physically or mentally capable of. If I tried to throw harder than I could, the ball went slower than normally. I couldn't force things, mentally or physically. If I couldn't fabricate conclusions in my mind about how to pitch to a batter, I didn't.

I let my catcher call the game and I just responded physically. Besides, if I surrender my mental load to the catcher, that's just one more thing I don't have to think about. When I tried to perfect everything, I perfected nothing."

For Seaver, more became less. The result was unpleasant. So he dealt solely within the framework of his limitations. He made peace with his limitations, not war. Most young pitchers develop in reverse of how Tom developed. They discover, by accident, and at an early age, that they possess a wondrous talent for throwing a baseball. A gift they didn't know they had, or how they got, or what it meant. So they just rode that talent without ever understanding it, how to control it, perfect it, not lose it. And when they did lose it, they had no clue how to recapture it because it was never their conscious creation.

When Tom's physical talent finally caught up to all the less tangible qualities he had been cultivating for years, he became the perfect pitcher at twenty-one. He possessed superior control, mental awareness, mental toughness, self-discipline, stamina, character, and now a blinding fastball he could throw wherever he wanted. He became the Six Million Dollar Man of pitching.

"That's why I appreciate my talent more than most," he says. "Some guys never appreciate the gift they have because they never consciously created it. They inherited it, which is why they never really possess it."

Tom is a big, muscular man, thick in his arms and shoulders and legs. Yet despite all the muscles his weightlifting had created, there are certain parts of Tom's body that are undeveloped. His waist is thick with excess fat. It is a constant source of kidding from Nancy. She will say, to Tom's embarrassment, "Thomas has an old man's waist, Pat. Really, he does! He is a lot like an old man, you know." Nancy's kidding doesn't really bother Tom. He knows a tightly muscled waist, rippling with abs, like mine, won't add anything to his pitching. In fact, it will distract from his pitching.

"I need that thick core," he says. "It gives me balance when I'm standing on one leg with my left leg raised."

Tom is not a vain man, like me. He would no more lift weights to sculpt an Adonis body than he would tell an obscene joke in public. He has no desire to call attention to himself, except for his pitching. If he is at all conscious of his physical image in public, it is only up to that point when it offends his own sense of propriety. He dresses neatly but indistinguishably in the clothes he receives from Sears, Roebuck and Company, to whom he is committed in business. Strangers who meet Tom remember his sandy hair, brown eyes, easy smile, his thick body, but can never remember what he was wearing at the time, unless it was his uniform.

The only thing Tom wants people to remember about him is his pitching. He wants the public to recognize his talent, but not the man who possesses it.

"After I won twenty-five games in sixty-nine, and the Cy Young," he says, "I became engulfed in a lot of publicity and recognition. It was like being caught up in a cloud. People who never met me were making judgments about me. Things were happening to me I had no control over. Then I had this fabulous realization—fabulous for me, anyway—that I had to cut all this stuff out of my life. I had to come back to myself, my pitching. Now I don't care about publicity, or what people say or write about me. I can relax and be what I am. And what I am is basically a dull guy. [Publicly, yes. Privately, no.] No one interviews me much anymore. Even my success is kinda dull. The sameness of it. At least it looks dull to others, not me. To me, it's fascinating.

"I used to think you could reach a point where success would be boring. But as I'm refining my pitching, I'm refining the pleasure I get from it. A victory used to give me pleasure. Then a well-pitched inning. Now I get great satisfaction from one or two pitches a game. I get in a situation where I have to apply everything I know, mentally and physically, on just one pitch. I think about what I should do and then make my body do it. That's a beautiful point to reach for an athlete. A light goes on in your head and you realize everything you've done in your life has been for this moment. There's no doubt in your mind that at this moment you can achieve perfection. It's a great thrill for me. Not a jubilant type of thrill, just a comforting satisfaction this is what you've devoted your life to."

⬟   ⬟   ⬟

An umpire joins us behind the batting cage at the Mets' spring training stadium. A trim, little man in a crisply pressed, dark-blue umpire's uniform. He has skin the color of mine, perpetually tanned even in winter, and a cherub's face. He waits until Tom and I finish talking, then he says something to Tom.

I lose myself in the rhythm of batting practice under a bright sun and a blue sky. I have always loved spring training. It's what I miss most about baseball. Always have ever since I left the game, or rather, the game left me. It's not the boringness of spring training I miss, the laziness, the same warm sun day after day, the same pale-blue sky, the grass always green, the Gulf and Atlantic waters always blue-green, like bad motel room art, the endless practices, the mindless repetition, the meaninglessness of the games that don't count, the total unreality of it all. A dreamscape. But what I do miss is that spring training sense that every year, beginning February 15, is a new beginning.

To this day I celebrate February 15 as the beginning of my new year, not January 1. A fresh start, new hope, endless possibilities that don't exist in the unchanging sameness of the real world. In the minors we used to call the real world "the lunch bucket brigade." The same shit job that never changes, holds no possibilities, is always the same, and then you die. I am grateful to God for giving me my second career as a writer. But sometimes, after staring at a blank piece of paper in a typewriter at my desk for five hours a day, seven days a week, twelve months a year since 1963, it drives me mad, until I type that first word onto paper. Then I feel exhilarated.

But it is not enough for me. All that interior satisfaction and none of the physical satisfaction I had as a pitcher. Like Tom, I am first a physical man. So I lift weights, enter bodybuilding contests, play manic three-man basketball games in a gym, all unsatisfying. I crave the physical pleasure and ego gratification I had as a pitcher. So I become self-pitying. I piss and moan. When Susie has had enough of my moods, she says, "Don't be a spoiled brat. Be grateful for what you have. Most people have no inner gratifications." She's right, as always. I feel ashamed. But in the recesses of my soul I still envy Tom Seaver for what he has, and I lost.

Behind the batting cage with Tom and the umpire, I watch the pitcher deliver the ball. The batter swings, a fly ball to left field. The infield coach to the right of the cage hits a ground ball to the shortstop. The left fielder circles the fly ball, pounds his glove. The shortstop scoops up the ground ball and throws to first base at the same moment the left fielder catches the fly ball. The pitcher reaches into a wire basket behind him and gets another ball. The first baseman stretches for the shortstop's throw, snaps it off the dirt disdainfully. The center fielder tosses the ball to the second baseman, who pantomimes a swipe at the imaginary runner sliding into the bag. The first baseman lobs the ball on two bounces to the infield coach. The batter takes a practice swing. The pitcher begins his motion…

Out of the corner of my eye I catch the umpire staring at me. He is still talking to Tom while he tries to remember me. His name is Terry Tata. He was an umpire in the Midwest League when I pitched for the Davenport, Iowa, Braves in 1960. We were both kids then. Nineteen, Italian-Americans from factory cities in Connecticut. We both felt adrift out there in Middle America, a strange, vast, silent plain of endless wheat fields and phlegmatic temperaments. After my games,

Terry and I would walk the streets of small towns, talking about our identical dreams. The strange people we'd been thrown among. "They don't show anything!" Terry said.

I said, "Who cares?"

At Davenport, in 1960, I lived in a boardinghouse run by a fat man and his wife and daughter. They called him "the Major." He didn't look like a major, not even a retired one. Although he did have a military man's gruff, booming voice, not to command but to be heard in a world of the deaf. His wife was soft-spoken. His daughter was a timid girl of nineteen, with an hourglass-shaped body. Her small eyes behind thick-lensed eyeglasses looked startled.

They lived on the first floor and rented out the four second-floor bedrooms to three transients and me. The transients were drifters, lean, haggard, silent men. They slept all day and were gone all night. I passed them on the stairway, my head lowered, returning from my games late at night. I saw one of them at a bar one night. He sat on a barstool, hunched over, while a woman standing behind him massaged his back. Suddenly his right fist shot over his shoulder and the women fell to the floor. No one noticed. They just stepped over her until she regained consciousness. A few weeks later, at the same bar, the same man was sitting on a barstool, the same woman, her left eye blackened, standing behind him massaging his back. I left quickly.

I never spoke to those transients and tried not to speak to the Major, sitting at night in an armchair in the living room off the hallway, watching television. But when he heard me come in, he called out, "IS THAT YOU, PAT? IS THAT YOU?"

"Yes, Major." I saw through the open door the Major's huge bulk in his armchair. His swollen legs and ankles.

He raised a beer can toward me and said, "Join me, Pat, for a beer."

I never did join him for a beer. Soon, he stopped asking. His wife, however, always said to me in a hushed voice, "Go join the Major, Pat. He'd like that." But I never did.

The Major and his wife and daughter came to all the games I pitched in Davenport. They sat behind the home plate screen. He cheered my every strike. And when I didn't throw strikes, walking batter after batter, and the fans began to boo me, I could hear only the Major's booming voice, "DON'T LISTEN TO THEM, PAT! YOU'RE DOIN' FINE, SON! YOU'LL GET IT!" Then I heard the Major's wife call out, "Listen to the Major, Pat. Don't worry." Only their daughter sat there silent, wearing white gloves, her hands folded on her lap.

One night, when I returned to their home after a disastrous performance, the Major met me in the hallway. He handed me the keys to his car and said, softly now, "Go for a ride, Pat. Take Marge if you'd like company." I sensed even then that he was not pushing his plain and timid daughter on me. He knew I had a girlfriend back home. He took pleasure in giving me her letters. Once when she telephoned from Connecticut when I was at the ballpark, he accepted the long-distance charges. He listened to her telling him I hadn't written her in weeks. He told her, "Don't worry, dear, he'll write. He's a fine boy." How did he know?

I'm sure the Major never intended for me and his daughter to have a romance. He just knew that Marge was shy and I was lonely and maybe for a moment together we could lighten our common solitude. So I took his car and his daughter that night and drove to the Mississippi River that ran past our ballpark, and parked. We walked along the riverbank in darkness and stared across the river at the lights of the nightclubs in Rock Island. We had little to say. We stopped and kissed now and then. She pressed her lips together and pressed them against my lips. Her arms, wrapped around my neck, held me tight, as if to protect her from drowning. After a kiss or two, I held her hand as we walked. She was wearing her white gloves even though it was a hot, humid night. Finally, she took them off. I felt her hand, the skin rough and scarred, as if it had been burned.

Driving back to her house, I asked her what branch of the service her father had been in. She said, "None. He's a major in the Salvation Army."

Standing behind the batting cage with Tom Seaver and Terry Tata, Terry reminded me of our days and nights together in the Midwest League when I was nineteen. But for some reason, Terry reminded me of the Major, too. At that moment I felt a fondness for the Major that I had never felt when he passed through my life years ago. Then, he was just a fat man I tried to avoid.

Unlike me, Terry had learned to control his Italian temper during games. He was a model of restraint behind the catcher. I was a madman on the mound, spewing fire like a dragon. Screaming, red-faced, when I thought Terry missed a pitch. "You fucking asshole!" I shouted halfway to the plate. "It was right down the cock!"

Terry came out from behind the catcher, his mask under his armpit, the way a Marine carries his dress hat. He held up his hands, palms out, as if to halt traffic. "Take it easy, Pat. It was a good two inches off the plate." But I wouldn't stop. He let me rage for a moment, knowing, like most Italians, that it meant nothing, except my frustration at my own failure. He smiled at me and said, "Are you finished?" I felt the fool. Put my head down. He tossed me a new ball. "Come on, *paisano*," he said. "Show me what you got."

And now, twelve years later, we are behind the batting cage in spring training, with the greatest pitcher in the game, who isn't me. Terry is a Triple A umpire hoping to make the Bigs this spring.

I am a writer now. Me! Who once had a better fastball than Tom Seaver's.

Terry leans across Tom and says to me, "Don't I know you? You look familiar."

I smile at him and say, "Yeah, Terry. Remember? The Midwest League in 1960."

A big smile spreads across his cherubic face. "Pat! Pat Jordan! Jesus! How are you doing?" And then, without thinking, Terry turns to Tom and says, "Tom, you shoulda seen this guy throw. They shoulda made a law against him, he threw so hard. He could bring it like you could only dream."

After Terry leaves, Tom, red-faced, accuses me of staging that little scene. I swear I didn't. Tom says, "You probably paid him fifty bucks to say that." He wasn't kidding! The prick! He has to diminish me because I had stepped onto his turf.

My face gets hot, too. I snap, "I didn't have to pay him shit. It's true." But Tom wouldn't believe me. That I could bring it faster than Tom Seaver. Which I could. Not much of an accomplishment compared to all of Tom's accomplishments, I admit. But it was mine. The sonuvabitch could at least acknowledge the possibility of it. He didn't have to have it *all*!

Tom told me once, so proud, that he had pitched a no-hitter in Little League. I said, "I pitched four no-hitters in a row in Little League. And two one-hitters." He flung his hand at me and said, "Bullshit you did."

I was a star in Little League. The Yankees invited me to be interviewed by Mel Allen on his pregame TV show when I was twelve. Dick Young wrote a column about me in the *Daily News*. I was in Ripley's *Believe It Or Not*, alongside a Zulu warrior with a bone through his nose. I pitched six games in my last year of Little League. People throughout New England drove for hours to watch me pitch. They came to see at least one batter get a hit off me. When one batter did hit a soft liner foul past third base, the fans gave him a standing ovation. He tipped his cap in appreciation. I struck him out on the next pitch, a fastball he never saw. As he walked back to his bench, I shouted at him, "Why don't ya tip your hat now?" They were boring games to watch. I struck out every batter I faced that year, except two. In high school I averaged over two strikeouts per inning for three years. Eighteen major league teams sent scouts to all my games. When I graduated, all eighteen came to my house. They hung around outside, leaning on their cars, talking, smoking cigarettes, while one at a time came into our house, sat on the edge of our sofa, and made their offers to my parents. They offered me money, more and more money, twenty, thirty, forty thousand dollars, until finally the Braves offered me enough.

I floated along on the cloud of my blinding talent until, in the minor leagues, I flew too close to the sun, fell out of the sky, and plunged to earth. I returned home to lug bricks up a scaffold for that mason. And while I did, I wondered, "Why?" What happened? I began to think about my talent, its loss, for the first time in my young life. Too late. For baseball anyway.

Batting practice is over for the Mets, and the Cardinals take the field for their BP. Tom and I walk over to the Iron Mike–branded pitching machine near the Mets bullpen, where a coach is waiting for him. Tom grabs a bat and steps into the cage to hit. Tom has been doing little more this spring than lift weights, run wind sprints, and hit in the cage because he is experiencing the first sore arm of his career. He can't understand how it happened. He had proceeded with his fifth spring training exactly as he had the previous four. When he felt the first sharp pain in his shoulder, he was confused. Then angry. Unable to throw, he took out his frustrations on Iron Mike.

Mike wheels, delivers a pitch. Tom slashes at the ball, "Aaaarrrggghhh!" A pop fly. Tom pounds the bat on the plate. Then he sets himself again, says, "Man on third. Two outs. A single drives in the winning run." Iron Mike delivers. Tom slashes a ground ball to short. "Damn it! Damn it! Damn it!"

Tom leaves the batting cage, drenched with sweat. He finds the Mets' team physician, Dr. Peter LaMotte. He raises his right arm over his head, digs the fingers of his left hand into that point where his arm, shoulder, and back meet, and says in a high-pitched, whining voice, "What *is* that?" Doctor LaMotte, a relaxed man who looks as if he's just come from the links, gives Tom a clinical explanation of his bruised muscles.

Tom's face clouds over with that exasperated look he gets when he has no interest in the turn of a conversation. He interrupts, "But I want…I want…I want it to feel…"

The doctor soothes away Tom's frustrations with more, less-clinical information. "Just a spring training sore arm," the doc says. "A little rest, it'll be fine."

Tom's voice loses its panic. Now it is curt and passionless, like a scientist's. Or a reporter's. Or a cop's, "Just the facts, ma'am." Tom says, "Which muscles are they? How did they get bruised? When will it be better? When can I throw?"

Later, Tom sits on his stool by his locker in the clubhouse while I stand over him. He says, "I don't know many parts of the arm, but I know these. The teres major. They'll heal with rest. They were bruised because I began throwing hard too soon. I hadn't taken into consideration I'm getting older. I can't proceed with spring training like I did at twenty-three. I've pitched almost fourteen hundred innings already. I have to be more cautious now."

Because he has a reporter's intelligence, Tom had to experience his sore arm first before he could figure out how to defend against it next time. A flaw in his nature. He is disinclined to intuit into the future without facts or experience because he does not trust abstractions, which he describes as "not the real world I live in." Abstractions are wispy, unmanly; they have no solid foundation. You can't see them, touch them, experience them in a physical way. It's only physical experience that is real to Tom. Like his experience watching those gulls. "Aren't they fascinating," he says. "I really could watch them fly all day. Or play dominoes with Nancy, or watch my daughter play with her toys. In the winter I like to get up in the morning and sit by the fire. What do I think about? How fabulous it is to watch wood burn." He laughs. "I don't dig deep like you. Life isn't that heavy for me. I leave a few weeds in my garden. Maybe I do it on purpose. I really don't know, though. I never think about such things."

● ● ●

On April 21, 1972, Tom Seaver defeated the Chicago Cubs, 2–0. It was his second consecutive shutout in as many starts, in a season barely two weeks old. His opponent was Burt Hooton, the rookie who had pitched a no-hitter only five days before. Against Seaver, Hooton was just short of brilliant. In seven innings, he allowed the Mets three hits, walked five, and struck out nine with his baffling knuckle-curveball. A performance worthy of high praise for a twenty-one-year-old rookie after his no-hitter, and the pressure of duplicating that effort against Seaver, the best pitcher in the game. His effort can best be described as a superior performance that, against Seaver, was sufficient enough to reward Hooton with internal satisfaction and a graceful loss. Seaver had been better. He didn't walk a batter in nine innings. He struck out nine, gave up four hits, no runs. His performance, which was brilliant, received less attention than Hooton's since it was expected of Seaver. Even after his spring training sore arm of eight weeks ago.

Two nights before that game, Seaver was scheduled to pitch against the Expos in Montreal. The game was rained out and he was rescheduled to pitch against Hooton two days later. When the Mets flew into LaGuardia Airport on the night of April 19, all of the players except one drove home. Seaver got a ride on the team bus to Shea Stadium, which was deserted in darkness. He went directly to his locker and put on his uniform. He filled a plastic bucket with baseballs and began the long walk across the field to the Mets' right-field bullpen. He looked like a weary old savage from prehistoric times, trudging through the danger of the night in that plodding, graceless walk of his, his head listing down to his right shoulder, on the hunt for sustenance.

When Seaver reached the bullpen, he began throwing baseballs against the home plate screen. His throwing was illuminated only by the lights from the parking lot. He warmed up quickly but carefully until he was throwing hard with great effort. His speed and control came slowly, only after much grunting and cursing in the darkness. Then he began to pitch to the imaginary Cub hitters he would face on April 21. Ernie Banks, Ron Santo, Billy Williams, all future Hall of Famers. He raised his arms over his head, turned sideways to the plate and raised his left leg, paused for a split second, his ball and glove cradled against his chest in prayer, his shoulders hunched around his head, for that "moment when I pull myself together, mentally and physically, to put everything I have into the pitch." Then he exploded toward the plate. He pitched until he was exhausted, accompanied only by the sound of baseballs rattling the screen, then dropping softly to the ground.

After Tom's shutout against Hooton and the Cubs, I called him the next morning to congratulate him on his performance. I said, "You didn't look like any sore-armed pitcher last night."

"No. I felt good." Then he told me how his throwing in the deserted Mets stadium on the night of April 19 had given him just the edge he needed.

"You're kidding," I said. "Why'd you do that?"

"It was my day to throw. I always throw on my day to throw."

● ● ●

Tom would finish the '72 season with a 20–10 record, a 1.76 ERA, and 289 strikeouts in 286 innings. After he retired from baseball fourteen years later, Tom said that his '72 season was the best pitching of his career.

CHAPTER THREE
1974

Tom is not pitching well. It is early summer of '74 and he has won only three games and lost five. His ERA is above three for the first time in his seven-year career.

I saw him pitch last night on TV, and it was dispiriting. He reminded me of myself years ago in the minor leagues. Great fastball, no control, and clueless. He threw as if he had no idea what he was doing, or where the ball would go, or how to get out of this terrible rut. It was not that he'd forgotten how to pitch entirely like I had; it was just that he seemed to panic in mid-delivery, his mind blank, and then rush the ball to the plate with as much effort as he could muster. He was trying to will everything, without thinking. After each hit, base on balls, line-drive out, he just grunted and tried to throw harder. He didn't pitch to his strength, his fastball, but nibbled around the plate with his slider until he got behind in the count and had to throw his fastball over the plate. He didn't set up batters for that one moment in a game "where I have to apply everything I know, mentally and physically, on just one pitch." There was no light going on in his head, no achieving perfection, just a constant state of doubt.

And the deeper he dug himself into a hole, the greater was his panic. I knew that panic well.

The next morning, I call him at home. "It's me."

"I figured I'd hear from you." No wise guy now, no sarcasm now, no "What the fuck do you know?" now. He's a mere mortal now.

"Now you know how I felt on the mound," I say.

"Yeah. I had no idea out there. I was just throwing, praying something would work. After each pitch I knew what I was doing wrong. But I couldn't make myself stop. It made me panic."

"Forget it," I say. "You're still throwing as hard as ever."

"It's my concentration I'm worried about, not my fastball."

"Don't dwell on it. It's baggage. Leave it at the station or you'll miss the next train out. You think too much about it and it'll fuck you up again. I should know."

"Now I can understand what happened to you. It must have been frightening."

"It was. Just make believe it never happened. Don't even think about it. Every bad game I had, I obsessed about it, worried it to death, which guaranteed I'd be worse my next game. Remember who you are. You're not me. You're Tom Fucking Seaver, the fucking greatest." He laughs. "Just repeat this to yourself. 'I'm Tom Seaver. I'm not Pat Jordan. I'm Tom Seaver. I'm not Pat Jordan.'"

Still laughing, he says, "Thank God for that."

We talk for a few more minutes, then he invites me to his house the next afternoon for lunch. "We can talk about it," he says.

When Tom is going well, he doesn't like to talk about his pitching. "I'm afraid I'll fuck it up," he says. But unlike most athletes, when he's going bad, he doesn't shrink from analyzing his pitching flaws. He believes most physical problems can be talked out. Understood. Resolved in his mind and then resolved physically.

I drive to Tom's house in my old 'Vette. I turn off the main road onto a narrow path wide enough only for a single car. The entrance to that path is unmarked, no street sign, and it's concealed by overhanging foliage so that it's virtually undetectable even to someone like me, who has been here before. The path is unpaved. Strewn with rocks, rutted by the snow and rain and the roots of tall trees. I can navigate that path with my ratty 'Vette only at a speed around five miles per hour. And still my 'Vette bounces and sags and creaks and its undercarriage bangs against the rocks and roots. To my left I see the sprawling eighteenth fairway of the Greenwich Country Club golf course, and to my right the woods. The branches of trees hang so low over the path that they brush against the hood of my car, scrape along its side, stick in through my open windows, as if to threaten. I come to a stone wall and a paved driveway that leads to Tom's converted farmhouse, and then a wall again and a line of trees that conceals the house until suddenly I am in front of it.

I see Tom sitting alone in the shadows on his porch. He is working a crossword puzzle in the *New York Times*. He is smoking a cigar. He leans back in his wicker chair and exhales to the sky, savoring the silence. It is broken only by a screen door slapping open, then shut, as Slider emerges from the house. Slider lies beside Tom. Absentmindedly, Tom scratches behind Slider's ears with his left hand. I get out of my 'Vette at noon of a sunny day. A softly undulating lawn surrounds the house on three sides. The grass is green, neatly trimmed, and bordered by thick foliage and tall trees that cast shadows over the lawn and completely obliterate from view the three houses that border Tom's property. He gets up to greet me. I comment on the seclusion.

Tom smiles and says, with a sweep of an arm, "They're there, but I can't see them. We're pretty well protected." He gestures toward the eighteenth fairway and says, "And nobody's gonna build on that."

Over the past seven years, Tom's success has grown so great that he now finds himself at a stage in his career when the only question asked of that career is how truly great will it be once he retires. With that success has come a public scrutiny Tom once embraced, then, after 1970, shunned. Over the next three years, his pitching flourished like his country garden. Two 20-win seasons, a 19-win season, and another Cy Young Award in 1973. His successes on the mound were so consistent that they actually became boring to his fans, who routinely expected of him, every game, only greatness.

Unwittingly, Tom began to play to his fans' demands for perfection from him. He let them know, through interviews, that he, too, expected perfection from himself. That he expected to become the greatest pitcher who ever lived. That his whole life was dedicated to that goal. He worked hard at it because it was the thing in his life he loved the most.

Now, three months into the '74 season, Tom was barely mediocre. His converted farmhouse in the woods is no longer a haven from public cheers and scrutiny, it's a refuge from public jeers. Tom is greeted with boos from Mets fans as he walks to the mound to start each game at Shea Stadium.

"Can you imagine?" he says to me. "I haven't thrown a pitch yet."

When he does throw a pitch, the boos get louder with each home run he surrenders. Fifteen so far to lead both leagues in a dubious category. The fans' rage becomes almost deafening when, with his head lowered, Tom walks off the mound in the middle of an inning, runs scored, runners on the bases. It's been a long dry spell for Tom since he's walked off the mound to cheers and a tip of his cap.

The rapaciousness and sometimes unrestrained glee with which fans greet Tom's latest failure is hard to comprehend since he does nothing to court it. He doesn't antagonize those booing fans, spit at them, give them the finger. He just hangs his head as if he sympathizes with their anger at him. He's let them down. He's angry at himself.

At times, the fans' fury with Tom can by truly frightening. One night I drove with him to Shea Stadium. He parked his Porsche in the players' private lot behind the right-field bullpen. He was instantly recognized by thirty or so fans standing behind the screen that separated them from the players. They began to shout that he was overpaid. Washed up. A bum. Their shouts became obscenities, grew more and more hysterical until it seemed they were going to climb the fence and physically attack him. Tom looked at me with raised eyebrows and said, "Do you believe it?" The fans gripped the wire fence in their fingers and shook it. The screen rattled in waves. I remembered from my college days those starving boys on a beach in *Suddenly Last Summer*. They, too, had rattled a screen to get at Cousin Sebastian before they devoured him.

● ● ●

"Can you believe it?" Tom says, reminding me of that scene now on the porch of his farmhouse. "That's got to be sick! One night it got so bad I charged the fence. They all scattered." He grins. It was something I would have done in my twenties. Had done, actually. I was backing into a parking space in downtown Bridgeport after circling the block for ten minutes. A little Volkswagen Beetle scooted into the space behind me. I got so furious, I went to the trunk of my car, took out a tire iron, and went back to the Beetle. I raised the tire iron to smash the cowering driver's windshield when some inner voice stopped me. My father's voice, saying in Italian that the curse of Italians was "*salvare la faccia*" (to save face).

"What would you have done if you got to them?" I say.

He shrugs, stops grinning. "I don't know." He is rocking in his chair, scratching behind Slider's ears. I am sitting on the porch railing. It is quiet except for the creaking of his rocking chair. Tom bangs forward in his chair and stops. He looks me in the eye and says, "Those people have never met me. Never said word one to me. They relate to an image, to that image's success which, in their own mind, they don't feel they have. That's not my fault. They have no conception of how hard I worked for my success. They resent it because they think it came easy to me. Nothing ever came easy to me. I worked to be happy. Those people never worked at it, never even asked themselves what would make them happy. Happiness is something they'll never attain, and that's not my fucking fault. They never sat down to think about it, what happiness is for them. It's always something one step beyond what they've got. It's never something they're doing at the moment. I'm happy rocking in this chair with my dog at this moment. I'm not thinking what's next that'll make me happy." He looks up at me and grins. "Well, maybe I am. Pitching well again will make me happy." Tom looks at his watch. "Time for lunch."

First, he lights the charcoal on his porch grill. Then we go into his kitchen. He hands me a beer from the refrigerator and takes one for himself. We sip our beers while Tom assembles the ingredients for our lunch. Two tomatoes. Two cucumbers. Two ears of corn. Some fresh mushrooms. One New York strip sirloin and one filet mignon. He goes outside and puts the steaks on his grill, then returns to the kitchen and arranges the vegetables on a wooden chopping block under a conical light. He begins slicing the mushrooms first. He works swiftly, with great concentration, like a professional chef. Chop-chop-chop-chop. When he speaks now, he looks up and stops chopping. When he's chopping, he looks down and is silent. He slices each mushroom into identical thin pieces in overlapping layers on the block. He puts them in a small cast-iron frying pan on the stove with a pat of butter. While they sizzle, he drops our corn into a pot of boiling water on the stove and sets a timer. Then he begins to slice the tomatoes. He stops slicing, looks up.

"To understand what's wrong with my pitching," he says, "you have to go back to last September." He holds the knife in front of his face as if it were a teacher's pointer. "I had a sore arm near the end of the season. My theory is, this spring training I was so conscious of not hurting my arm again that I never pushed it very hard. When the season began, my arm was fine, but it wasn't very strong. I couldn't pop the ball. So I tried to throw harder than I was capable of."

"You broke your own cardinal rule," I say. "Never try to do something you're not able to on any given day."

"Thank you," he says. "As if I don't know that *now*. But that wasn't the only thing." He goes back to slicing his tomatoes. When they are both evenly sliced, he looks up again.

"I also found out my legs weren't in pitching shape either. I'd never really driven with them off the mound in spring training. I get my fastball as much from my legs as my arm. So I got whacked around pretty good the first couple of games until I realized what was wrong. Then, against Frisco, I started driving hard with my legs again and I pitched a shutout. In my next start, against the Dodgers, I struck out sixteen in eleven innings, even though I didn't get the win. Now I figured everything is all right again. Then, boom, I get beat twice by the Cubs, four-three. I lost one of those games because of two broken-bat singles over the infield. The other game I lost I got no breaks."

Tom sees me about to speak. He shakes his head no and waves the knife in the air. "I know, I know," he says. "No excuses. I have a theory about that. When you're not throwing well, bad breaks become glaring and significant. When you're throwing well, they become insignificant because you overcome them and win the game despite them. They don't matter. They only matter to guys not throwing well. That was me."

He goes back to slicing the cucumbers. Chop-chop-chop. He stops and looks up, waving his knife. "And those broken-bat singles? Some guys say there's nothing you can do about them. But I don't agree. If I was really throwing well, those little flares to the outfield would never have reached the outfield. They'd be pop-ups to the infield. See what I mean?" He smiles at his own conclusion. "My fastball was maybe this much less than it was last year." He holds up the thumb and forefinger of his left hand an inch apart. "I was that far off. Those games in Frisco and LA had deceived me into thinking I'd got it back in two starts. Well I hadn't. So now I figure I'm about four starts from midseason form. But I'm satisfied with my progress. I'm not getting whacked anymore. I'm just not pitching as well as I'm capable of."

He finishes slicing the cucumbers and arranges them and the tomatoes on two separate plates. He spreads the slices around one half of each plate precisely as a card player would fan out a deck of cards, each slice overlapping the next. He looks at the plates and smiles. Then he picks each of the corncobs from the boiling water with tongs and puts one on each plate.

"Oh, damn!" he says. "I forgot the steaks!" He runs to the porch and calls out, "They're OK. They're not burnt." He comes back with the steaks on a big platter and puts it on the kitchen's farm table. "I was talking so much I forgot all about them."

We sit down to eat. Tom puts the filet mignon on my plate and the sirloin on his. He says, "That's the biggest fucking filet I ever saw." It's the size of a football.

We pick our corn, tomatoes, and cucumbers off their plates and arrange them on our steak plates. Tom gets up and gets us both beers. When he sits back down, he says, "It's just a momentary thing. My fastball's gotta come back. I'm only twenty-nine! Nothing hurts!… But maybe it won't. I've thought of that, too. I might have to make some changes in my pitching. Keep the ball down more, less high fastballs, more off-speed pitches, sinkers, maybe brush back the hitters a little, something I never had to do before. I don't like to do that. The ball could slip out of my hand, maybe hurt someone. I've always had enough velocity to get batters out by throwing the ball over the plate. See if they can beat me. Up to now, they couldn't." He shrugs.

We eat in silence for a few moments. Then Tom says, "They say when you get older you have to make adjustments. Maybe that's one of them. I can't do things with my fastball I could before. There are other things, too."

I wait a moment, then say, "What other things?"

He flashes me a sly grin. "I'm keeping those to myself."

"Like what? A spitball?"

He laughs. "You think?" Then he says, "All in all this has been a very frustrating period for me. For a while I just didn't want to talk about it. After one of my Chicago losses, I was so mad I wouldn't talk to the writers after the game. The next day a writer comes up to me and says, 'If you lose your next game are you gonna talk to us?' Christ, can you imagine that? He thought I planned such things. Like I'd already made that decision before I pitched. It was just an emotional thing. No matter how hard I try to control my emotions, sometimes I can't. I've kicked over my share of water coolers and trash cans and training tables. I'm not *that* calculating!"

During Tom's years with the Mets, he has mostly gotten along with sportswriters. He was always a player they could turn to for a willing and articulate analysis of his pitching, himself, his teammates, in precise, objective, and some might say "prissy" terms. So far this season, however, he has had more than his share of difficulties with writers. After another dispiriting loss, when he refused to talk to them, they criticized him in their columns. He was spoiled by too much success, and now in adversity he was not so eager to expound on his pitching.

Like those rabid fans, the writers seemed to derive more than a hint of satisfaction from Tom's failures. They wrote that, at twenty-nine, his career was on its downswing. He'd never again be the dominating pitcher he once was. "Times have changed," wrote one columnist. "There were times when Tom Seaver would pitch a shutout and then talk about how he should not have given up three hits." The columnist went on to write that Seaver is more realistic about his talent now. Like the rest of us, he no longer expects to be perfect. He is just happy now to win a modestly well-pitched game.

There is something about Tom Seaver that gives rise to envy in the rest of us. But that envy is not for his success, or his talent, or his money, or his fame, or his lifestyle. It is envy for the obvious satisfaction he derives from those things. He too glibly articulates that satisfaction in a world of inarticulate people. He is too content in a world of discontented people. His standards are too lofty in a world of people who cannot meet their most minimal standards. His life is too orderly and disciplined and prescribed in a world of people whose daily lives border on chaos. He is too simplistically rational about such tasks as pitching a baseball while around him most people are rendered irrational by life's momentous complexities. Tom Seaver has ocular block, a tunnel vision that focuses on any single, simple task at a moment in his life. Around him are people whose concentration is diffused, rendered impotent by a thousand overwhelming tasks.

In all the years I've known Tom, our conversations have always been about him, his pitching, his arm, his salary, his life. He has never asked about my life, my work, my aspirations. It has never dawned on him that this might not be the natural order of life. That everything doesn't revolve around him. He just assumes this as a given, his athlete's blessing.

🏠   🏠   🏠

Before I leave his house after lunch, Tom says to me, "If people get pleasure out of knocking me, what can you say about them? I really don't care what people think about me. In my own mind I don't consider myself a public figure. I don't read the newspapers anymore. I mean, I can't control what they write about me, so why bother? I feel no pressure from the fans, or writers, or anyone. I don't live in their world. I live in my own world." He gestures with his arm at the woods that protect his house from others. "I live in the real world."

🏠   🏠   🏠

Tom ends the season with the worst record of his career. He wins 11 games and loses 11, with a 3.20 ERA, the highest of his career. But it is an aberration. By '75, he's Tom Seaver again. "Tom Terrific," the fucking greatest. He finishes that season with a 22–9 record and a 2.38 ERA.

CHAPTER FOUR
1977

In the late spring of 1977, I wasn't paying much attention to Tom Seaver's career. The boring sameness of his successes had started to bore even me. I no longer had the time, inclination, or interest in following the dramas in the life of a wealthy, famous baseball pitcher who was not me. I had very real problems in my own life. A failing marriage, troubled children, and the loss of my rabbi, Ray Cave, as my editor at *Sports Illustrated*. Ray had advanced to a new role at Time-Life Inc. My new editor, who replaced him, was not much interested in what I was writing for *SI*. It was my first real lesson as a professional freelance writer. I thought I had been writing for *Sports Illustrated*. But I wasn't. I was writing for Ray Cave. Now, with Ray gone ("Go there and tell me what you see, Pat"), whenever my new editor, who had been a writer at *SI*, assigned me a story he gave me an outline to follow, with bullet points for what he wanted in the story. I knew instinctively that it was his way of telling me my days at the magazine were numbered. So I began hustling assignments from *Playboy*, *People*, *Time*, *Life*, *Reader's Digest*, *Geo*, and eventually *Newsweek's* *Inside Sports*, in anticipation of the future I knew was coming. A career without *SI*. If I had paid more attention to Tom's career that year, I would have seen that he was being forced to confront that same future. Life without the Mets. But that possibility was inconceivable to Tom at the time.

In January 1976, Tom began contentious contract negotiations with the Mets' GM, Joe McDonald, and board chairman, M. Donald Grant. For most of his career, Tom had negotiated his own contracts with the Mets, with often unpleasant results. He created acrimony with executives he dealt with, and often after he signed the contract he wanted, he would find out he had undersold himself in comparison to other pitchers. In this case, he had a figure for his services so locked in his mind that he barely noticed that seismic changes were on the horizon of baseball's salary structure.

Tom informed the team's president, Lorinda de Roulet, that he expected to be the first pitcher to receive at least a $200,000-a-year contract. She responded, "Over my dead body." Ms. de Roulet was still breathing, however, in February 1976, when Tom signed a three-year contract with the Mets for $225,000 a year, the highest salary ever for a pitcher at that time. But not for long.

By the spring of 1977, MLB had abandoned its reserve clause, which had bound players to their teams at the owners' whim. The players either signed contracts owners offered them, were traded or released, or sat out the season cashing unemployment checks from Uncle. (I pitched in the minors with a veteran minor league shortstop, ten years older than me, who lived the off-season in Buffalo, New York. In December each year, he'd go to the state unemployment office. One time the functionary behind the desk asked him what kind of job he was looking for. The shortstop looked out the window at the falling snow, then turned back to the functionary. He said, "Shortstop mostly. Maybe some second base. If necessary, third base, too. But that would be my last choice.")

Some players got part-time jobs selling used cars. Or, if they were famous enough, greeting gamblers in Vegas casinos. But now, without the reserve clause in 1977, players could become free agents after each contract they signed expired. They could then offer themselves to other teams in what was essentially an auction.

Less than a year after Tom signed what he thought was a historic contract, he looked around the pitching landscape to discover some very good, but not great pitchers, like himself, and even mediocre pitchers, were signing contracts he never envisioned. One of his flaws. Tom didn't like to intuit events before they happened. He preferred to deal with those events only when they became a reality. Now the reality was he was vastly underpaid.

The Yankees signed Catfish Hunter, a terrific pitcher but no Tom Seaver, to a five-year, $3.35 million contract. The last three years of that contract, Catfish won 23 games and lost 24. In 1977, the Atlanta Braves signed Andy Messersmith, a very good pitcher, to a three-year, $1 million contract. He went 7–11 over those three years, and retired. In 1977, Wayne Garland, a less than mediocre pitcher, with a career won-lost record of 55–66, signed a ten-year, $2.3 million contract with the Cleveland Indians. Over the first five years of that contract he won 28 games and lost 48. For the last five years of that contract he was out of baseball but still being paid.

No wonder Tom was pissed off. But he should have been pissed off at himself for not having the patience, and foresight, to wait until free agency before he renegotiated his $225,000-a-year contract with the Mets. I was pissed off at him, too, for not having the patience he always chided me that I didn't have.

Tom had an excellent a season in '76 (14–11, 2.59 ERA, 235 Ks, 221 hits in 271 innings), which might have been a 20-win season if the Mets were not so punchless. That Mets team rarely scored even a minimal number of runs for Tom in his games. In one seven-game stretch he gave up an average of less than two runs per game and ended up with four losses and three no decisions. Now wonder then, in the spring of '77, that Tom began a merciless drumbeat in the press accusing the Mets' front office of being cheapskates who refused to bid big money for talented free agents like Gary Matthews. By "the Mets," Tom meant the patrician, Wall Street, Mets chairman, M. Donald Grant, his nemesis. Grant had already called Seaver an "ingrate" during the '76 negotiations, and even a "communist" because of his demands that teams (i.e., the Mets) pay decent salaries to their "workers" (which, I don't believe, was precisely what Marx had in mind when he wrote "Workers of the world unite!"). When Seaver joined the Greenwich Country Club, Grant accused him of trying to rise above his station (as a proletariat worker?) by having the gall to join a country club Grant himself was a member of.

Grant also implied that Seaver was using his criticism that the Mets were skinflints in pursuing free agents as nothing more than a smoke screen for his own greedy attempts to now renegotiate his 1976 contract. Tom said that "my unhappiness [with the Mets] started with the negotiations of ['76]." By May 31, 1977, Tom was referring to his dealings with Grant as "deteriorated beyond repair." Grant enlisted in this pissing contest *Daily News* sports columnist Dick Young, whose son-in-law, Thornton Geary, worked in the Mets' front office, thanks to Young's intervention with Grant. Young wrote on June 1 that even if the Mets wanted to trade Seaver, "Nobody wants [him]." Young parroted Grant's complaints in his column that Seaver "had destroyed the market [for himself]" because he was "a headache" and was an "irreparably damaging destructive force on the Mets."

The possibility that the Mets might try to trade Seaver was unthinkable to fans and most New York columnists whose names were not Dick Young. Maury Allen of the *New York Post* wrote that "one does not dispose of a Picasso." Young responded that no other teams wanted Seaver with "a pacifier" in his mouth.

In a last-ditch effort to forestall what now seemed a possibility—Tom leaving the Mets—Tom called de Roulet, the team's president, on June 14, 1977. By the time he got off the phone with her, Tom was assured that the person who'd once told him she'd pay him $200,000 a year "over my dead body" had agreed to sign him to a new contract for $1.1 million over three years. Tom went to sleep that night relieved that his dark nightmare was over. He woke the next morning in his Atlanta hotel room and went down to breakfast. He bumped into his Greenwich neighbor, Dick Schaap, in the lobby. Schaap asked him if he'd read Dick Young's *Daily News* column this morning. Tom said he couldn't find a *Daily News* in the lobby. So he called the Mets and had someone there read it to him.

Young's column compared Tom to Dodgers owner Walter O'Malley, whose reputation as a money-grubbing carpetbagger was based on his Dodgers abandoning blue-collar Brooklyn for the glitz and sunshine and lucre of LA. "Both are very deceptive," Young wrote, "[and] both are very greedy." Then Young accused Tom of wanting to appear "that he wanted [the Mets] to spend [money]" on other players, "but he really wanted it to be spent on himself," but he "couldn't say that out loud…. How would it look for Tom Terrific, All-American Boy, to disavow a contract he had signed in good faith?" Then he impugned Tom's manhood, writing, "Tom Seaver is jealous of those who had the guts to play out their option or used the threat of playing it out as leverage for a big raise…. He talks of being treated like a man. A man lives up to his contract." (A few years after he wrote this, Young broke his contract with the *Daily News* for more money with the *New York Post*.)

Young saved his coup de grâce for last. He implied that Tom's wife was secretly jealous that Nolan Ryan's wife had more money to spend shopping than she did because Nolan was making more money ($300,000 a year to Tom's $225,000) than her husband. At which point Tom went ballistic at Young for bringing his wife into his squabble with the Mets. He called the Mets in a fury and told them, "Get me out of here!" It's probably something I would have done if I was in Tom's place. *Salvare la faccia*, the curse of Italians, and, it seems, certain white breads named Tom Seaver.

The Mets obliged Tom, trading him that day to the Cincinnati Reds for a packet of mediocre players, who could not stop the Mets from losing over 95 games a year for the next five of six years. The Mets were so bad that fans stayed away in droves. For five years after Tom's banishment, the Mets averaged under a million fans a year, the tenth-worst attendance of twelve teams in the National League. Shea Stadium was dubbed "Grant's tomb," and M. Donald Grant himself was called "the chairman of the bored."

Grant's son, Michael, described his father years later, saying, "They [the media] pictured him as a member of the elite moneyed class, a stuffed shirt. He was anything but. He was a guy that came to this country [from Canada] in the Depression and made his way. He never even graduated from high school."

Grant arrived in New York City as a twenty-year-old immigrant with less than $100 in his pocket. He got a job as a night clerk in a hotel and picked up some change moonlighting as a part-time hockey referee. But he was a handsome man, who may not have been born a patrician (his grandfather was a blacksmith), but he looked like one. Which eventually attracted the attention of a wealthy socialite, Alice Waters. Grant was twenty-eight when they married. Immediately, Grant's name began to appear regularly in the *New York Times* society columns, which led to a job on Wall Street and his own wealth.

Grant was the administrator, not a broker, for the offices of Fahnestock & Co., and eventually became a partner in the firm. He was described as a "young man with something on the ball," who "ran a tight ship at Fahnestock. He keeps his costs down...and pays the young guys the least he can get away with." Now, like a born patrician, Grant joined hunt clubs and squash clubs and the Greenwich

Country Club. When he ran the Mets in the '70s, he enjoyed taking his important Wall Street friends down to the clubhouse so he could introduce them to his "boys."

Over the years, like the good son, Michael Grant tried to defend his father's handling of the Seaver fiasco. He said once, "He felt bad he was labeled a villain. He thought he had done well by Seaver. He thought...Seaver had traded himself. It was just sad that in his waning days while he was still chairman, he needed a bodyguard to walk around Shea Stadium."

A year after what became known as "the Midnight Massacre" (other "greedy" Mets players were also banished, to teams other than the Reds), M. Donald Grant was fired.

When Dick Young was enshrined in the writers' wing of the Baseball Hall of Fame in 1978, he was booed by fans. He laughed at them. He claimed for years that it never bothered him that his sportswriting career was never again defined by his columns after June 16, 1977. Young would always be remembered by New Yorkers only as the man who drove Tom Seaver out of New York and "left behind a diminished city," wrote *Post* columnist Pete Hamill.

In the September 1977 issue of *Harper's Magazine*, A. Bartlett Giamatti, a Renaissance literature scholar who'd become the president of Yale from 1978 to 1986, wrote a much-praised essay about what Tom Seaver meant to baseball, the Mets, New Yorkers, and the country. And, most importantly, what Tom Seaver meant to him as a baseball fan. It was titled: "Tom Seaver's Farewell. There is no joy in Gotham."

Giamatti wrote that Tom and Nancy Seaver's tearful leaving of Shea Stadium and New York City after the Midnight Massacre generated in him the same "inflated cognition" and outsized feelings of intense anguish that he felt when viewing Masaccio's fresco *The*

Expulsion from the Garden of Eden. "Clearly evil had entered the world," Giamatti wrote.

Tom and Nancy, Adam and Eve. Dick Young and Donald Grant vying for the role of the Snake. Tom Seaver's pride, the Big Apple. New York City, the Garden of Eden…in the '70s? Garbage and transit strikes, blackouts, hookers and peep shows on Broadway? The Son of Sam?

Giamatti then expressed his belief that Tom Seaver's "dignitas" and "artisan's dignity" and his "cluster of virtues seemingly no longer valued…transcends even the great and glorious game, and that such a man is to be cherished, not sold."

The problem with Giamatti's sentiments about Seaver and baseball is that he was, like most fans and fellow dilettante sportswriters like Roger Angell and George Will, clueless about both the game and the men who played it.

Giamatti's fevered worship of Seaver was based, in good part, on "the only time I ever met Seaver," he wrote. It was in 1971, at a gathering of the Seavers, the Schaaps, and himself at the New York apartment of Erich Segal, "then at the height of his fame as the author of *Love Story.*" Here's how Giamatti remembers that night in his *Harper's Magazine* essay:

> The talk was light, easy, and bright, and was produced almost entirely by the Schaaps, Nancy Seaver, and Segal…. I was content to listen and watch Seaver. He sat somewhat apart, not, I thought, by design, not, surely, because he was aloof, but because it seemed natural to him. He was watchful, though in no sense wary, and had that attitude I have seen in the finest athletes and actors (similar breeds), of being relaxed, but not in repose, the body being completely at ease but, because of thousands of hours of practice, always poised, ready at any instant to gather itself together and move. Candid in his gaze, there was a formality in his manner, a gravity, something autumnal in the man who

played hard all summer. He sat as other men who work with their hands sit, the hands clasped chest high or folded in front of him, often in motion, omnipresent hands that, like favored children, are the objects of constant, if unconscious attention and repositories of complete confidence.

Giamatti's mythologizing essay about a man he met only once, and then was so tongue-tied in that man's presence that he didn't remember a word either of them had spoken, so impressed baseball's owners that, in 1988, they elected Giamatti to be the seventh commissioner of Major League Baseball. He died of a heart attack on September 1, 1989, at age fifty-one, just five months after taking office.

◆ ◆ ◆

Tom Seaver left the Mets on June 15, 1977, with a 7–3 won-lost record. He went on to win 14 games and lose 3, with a 2.34 ERA, with the Reds for the rest of that season. That was his fifth and last 20-win season. Years later, he would tell me that going to the Reds was the best thing that could have happened to his career at that time.

CHAPTER FIVE

1982

In the late spring of 1982, I fly to Cincinnati, where Tom is still pitching for the Reds. When I get off the plane, a woman, not my wife, is waiting for me in the airport terminal. She drives me to my hotel and sits in the lobby, reading a newspaper, while I check in at the front desk. A businessman sitting across from her smiles at her. She ignores him. Then she follows behind me as I walk to the elevator.

When we get to my room, I tell her I have to go out for a few hours to talk to Tom.

"Can I go with you?" she says.

"I don't think so."

"Why not?"

"It's business."

"No problem. I'll talk to his wife."

"She's not here yet. She's back in Connecticut with their daughters. They're still in school."

"But I was looking forward to meeting him."

"I know. I'm sorry. But he wouldn't understand."

"He's a ballplayer, isn't he? They all have girlfriends on the road."

"Not Tom. He's not like other ballplayers." I can't tell her the real reason why she can't come with me. I don't want Tom to think less of me for being with a woman not my wife. I don't know why that matters to me, but it does.

"We'll go out to dinner when I get back," I say. "Someplace nice. You make reservations."

She smiles at me. "Of course. It's business. I understand."

"I'll make it up to you," I say.

"Here," she says. She hands me the keys to her car. "No sense paying for a taxi."

● ● ●

Tom and I are on the redwood deck in the back of his condominium only a few yards from the third tee of the Jack Nicklaus-designed golf course in Mason, Ohio, a suburb thirty minutes from Cincinnati. Through a line of trees I see a steady parade of golf carts putt-putting up the fairways in agonizing slow motion. They remind me of those little white carts in the TV serial *The Prisoner*, with Patrick McGoohan. The men in the golf carts are wearing pastel-colored sweaters and garishly checked pants.

I am shirtless in the hot sun. I am half sitting, half lying on a lounge chair, my eyes closed, my face to the sun, catching some rays for my tan. Tom, his cheek swollen with a wad of tobacco, is kneeling on the deck, hunched over a line of flowerpots. He is wearing a plaid shirt and chino pants as he plants, with great care, his geraniums, begonias, and impatiens in clay pots. When I first drove up to his condo an hour ago, Tom met me in the parking lot. He got in the woman's car with me before I could park it and said, "Come on. I have to get some things." Then he looked around inside the car, a small Toyota that looked lived in. A box of tissues on the floor. Cigarette stubs in the ashtray, a Styrofoam coffee cup in the console, both with lipstick smudges on them. I closed the ashtray and laid my small shoulder bag with my wallet, notebook, and pens in it over the console.

"Where the hell did you get this thing?" he said. "Rent-A-Wreck?"

"It's the only one they had," I said. "They wanted to clean it for me. I said don't bother, nobody important's gonna be in it."

"Why didn't you ask them if they had a gold Corvette with a T-top that leaks? And a defroster that doesn't defrost." I glanced at him. He shrugged, palms out. "Just asking. Do you still have that thing?"

"Of course. It's a collector's item now. Worth more than your Porsche."

"I'll bet."

He made me drive him to a nursery, where he painstakingly went up and down the aisles of a greenhouse, searching for plants.

"This is boring," I said.

Without looking up at me, he said, "To you, maybe. Not me."

"Is this how you spend your day off?"

"Absolutely. It's my pleasure."

Back at his condo, I had to help him carry all the plants to his back deck, where he is now repotting them. "Why don't you just leave them in the pots they came in?" I ask.

He glances back at me and says, "That's what you would do."

"No. I wouldn't get them in the first place."

He harrumphs and goes back to his replanting. He kneads the dirt in the pots with his hands. "This is a joy to me," he says. "Some people, like you, would see it as drudgery. But I love it. My daughters will love all the colors when they finally get here." Tom spits some tobacco juice into the dirt of a begonia plant. "I put in a rusty nail, too," he says. "The iron is good for the soil." He glances back at me again and says, "You really give a shit, huh?"

"Remind me again why I spent eight hours of my life on planes, trains, and automobiles to get here just to watch you pot flowers."

"You love it. You just won't admit it."

"Right." I close my eyes to the sun. Tom keeps repotting his flowers. He pulls them out of their small plastic pots, gives them a shake to get off dried dirt, then puts them into bigger clay pots filled with black potting soil so they have more room to grow.

Nancy and their two daughters won't arrive from Connecticut for another few weeks after school gets out. Until then, Tom leads the life of a bachelor. He hates it. He hates it even more when he is not pitching well. So far, this season has been the worst of his career. He has lost five games and hasn't won one. His ERA is over five runs per game. It seems, like a bad penny, I always appear on his doorstep when he is not pitching well. Maybe it's a compliment to me that he'll never admit to. I think he likes analyzing his pitching with me when he's going bad. He once asked me why I never became a pitching coach. I told him, "Because nobody asked." When I saw him pitch a game on TV a week ago, I called him and told him what his problem was.

"You're thirty-eight," I said. "You no longer have that great fastball."

He said, "Tell me something I don't know."

"You can't get by anymore with just hard stuff that's not so hard anymore. Fastball, slider. You need a good curveball as an off-speed pitch."

"How many times do I have to tell you, I never understood the concept of a curveball."

"It's your motion," I said. "Drop and drive. You get too low to the ground to be able to get your arm up for an overhand curve."

"It's too late to change that now, Big Guy," he said.

Now, on the deck of his condo, he says, "I have lost a little off the fastball. But my control is off, too."

I tell him what Warren Spahn told me when I went to spring training with the Braves in 1960. I was eighteen, Spahnie was forty. He told me, "People who don't know always think the arm goes first when you get to forty. But it's always the legs that go first. If I had a forty-year-old arm and twenty-year-old legs I could pitch forever.

It's when the legs go that prevents a pitcher from throwing the ball where he wants to."

Tom looks up from his potting. "Spahn was right. I had a pulled thigh muscle this past spring training. It hindered my progress. Then I got the flu." He shakes his head. "It was depressing, dealing with that stuff. Then I got here and didn't pitch well. I was miserable. But it's not only my pitching. When my family's not with me, there's no escape from adversity, or loneliness. If I come home after a bad game and my daughters want to go to the swimming pool, I don't tell them no because I'm pitching badly. I take them. They don't care about my pitching that much. They're kids. They have more positive things in their lives. They make me forget myself."

Tom says he thinks he injured the thigh muscle the previous winter when he threw in the cellar of his Greenwich farmhouse. "The cellar floor is concrete," he says. "It's not the same as throwing off a dirt mound. You use different muscles. Next winter I'm gonna build a dirt mound down there."

I don't ask him why he didn't anticipate such an injury now that he's thirty-eight. If I did, he'd just tell me he'd thrown off that cellar floor for years and never had a problem. Tom doesn't like to anticipate problems before they happen so he can prevent them. To Tom, anticipating problems before they happen brings bad luck. He doesn't like to operate in a world of possibilities. Like he says, he lives in the Real World, a concrete world of experiences, not hypotheses. He has to experience things first before he can adjust to them.

From 1975 to 1981, Tom has averaged over 16 wins a season. He was 22–9 in '75, 21–6 in '77, and 14–2 in a strike-shortened '81 season, one of the best seasons of his career. He would have won his fourth Cy Young Award after '81, if the Dodgers' young Mexican pitcher, Fernando Valenzuela, hadn't been such a sentimental favorite. The consensus among CYA voters was that Tom had already won his fair share of awards, so why not give it to this young pitcher with the effervescent personality? Furthermore, Seaver was old news, a dull interview, and a scold to sportswriters half the time, even if he had been by far the best pitcher in baseball last year. Now, a year later, it's as if that '81 season never existed for Tom who, at thirty-eight, bears no relation to himself as a thirty-seven-year old pitcher.

Tom says it didn't bother him that he was deprived of his fourth CYA last year. Nor does it bother him being underpaid. He will earn about $400,000 in '82, while teammate Tom Hume, a pedestrian pitcher with a lifetime 39–37 record, will make almost $600,000. Tom's only goal left in baseball is to win 40 more games and join a handful of pitchers who have won 300 or more games in a career.

"If I don't get it, I don't get it," Tom says. "It doesn't really bother me. It's like being underpaid. So what? I didn't think salaries would go as high as they did. But I'm financially secure. How much money do you need? It's good to have goals, but sometimes you lose sight of what the initial enjoyment is if you worry about goals. It's like the other night. I was driving home from the ballpark listening to the radio. They had this interview with an oboist for the Minneapolis Symphony Orchestra. He was retiring, so they asked him if he had any advice for young musicians. He said, 'Remember, no matter how long you work, don't forget what made you do it. Love of music.' When I have to leave the game, I won't panic. I won't worry about recognizing when it's time either. I'll know. I won't be able to pitch. I'll have to find other satisfactions. Cerebral ones. Still, I'll have to supplement them with some kind of physical activity. Do you know, in the midst of the Falkland Crisis, Alexander Haig was playing tennis?"

Yet Tom Seaver is a prideful man. Despite his protestations to the contrary, it was money that precipitated the most profound change in his career in 1977. I think that experience exhausted him. It also made him gun-shy, I think, about always negotiating his own contracts. He was getting older. That experience punctuated that point. Like his diminishing fastball is making a point to Tom now. Nothing stays the same. Sooner or later you have to adjust to age. And with it a loss of energy, a diminishment of will, a loss of heart. Tom couldn't do all the things he used to do. Donald Grant and Dick Young wore him down, like Joe Frazier wore down Muhammad Ali after their last fight. Even though Ali won that fight, he was never the same fighter again. I don't think the residual effects of that 1977 contract struggle ever left Tom after it was over. When Tom and Nancy finally settled in Cincinnati, Nancy said, "Is it over now?" Tom replied, "I think it's just beginning."

"I'll tell you one thing," Tom says. "I was lucky the Mets traded me to the Reds five years ago. If I was still with the Mets, the kind of team they've got, I never would win three hundred games." When the Mets traded Tom to the Reds early in the 1977 season, he had a 7–3 record with the Mets and finished with a 14–3 record with the Reds, for a combined 21–6. Over the five years from '77 to '81, when Tom pitched for the Reds, they averaged 24 more victories per season than the hapless Mets. That's one reason why Tom has to win only 40 more games to become one of a handful of pitchers to win 300 games or more in a career.

"It was all Dick Young's doing," Tom says. "He wanted me out of New York, and he got his wish."

"You should send him a thank-you card," I say. Then I tell Tom my Dick Young story.

In the late '70s, I was invited to speak to a sports journalism class at the University of Delaware. When I arrived at the airport, the journalism professor picked me up and drove me to an expensive hotel where he had booked a room for me. It was already 7:00 p.m. I had eaten an early dinner at LaGuardia Airport. I was tired. All I wanted to do was sleep, get up at 5:00 a.m., have my coffee, speak to his journalism class at 9:00 a.m., and be back on a plane to LaGuardia before noon.

I looked at the hotel from his car and said, "How much is this costing the school?"

He said, "Five hundred dollars."

"For ten hours? That's a waste. Save the money and put me up at a guest room in the dorm. Just point me to the cafeteria for coffee in the morning, and from there, to your classroom."

He tried to talk me into the hotel room, but I wouldn't have it. The next morning, I woke at 5:00 a.m. in a guest room in the dorm, found the cafeteria, had my coffee, and walked to his classroom by eight. No one was there, so I waited outside, smoking my cigar, and watching the students hustle to their early morning classes.

After I spoke to his class, the young professor drove me to the airport. Along the way he told me that the last guest speaker to his class was Dick Young. "He insisted I have a suite for him at the hotel," the professor said. "The next morning, he didn't show up at my class on time, so I went to the hotel and knocked on his door. Young opened the door wearing only his boxer shorts. I could see a naked woman on his bed inside. She must have been thirty years younger than him." He gave me a thin smile. "Obviously, she wasn't his wife of forty years. I literally had to drag him to my class an hour late for his talk."

Tom laughs at my story and shakes his head. I say, "The moral conscience of sport. Getting some nookie on the side." I did not add, "Like me."

Late in the afternoon, after Tom finishes his repotting, he sits with me on the deck. We watch the old men golfers putter by. Suddenly, Tom perks up. He sees three young Reds teammates, in their twenties, about to tee off. Tom jumps up. "Watch this!" He sneaks onto the rough and hides behind a tree. He peeks out with an evil smile, like a comic book villain, as one of the players tees up his drive. Tom waits until he is on his downswing before he lets out a bloodcurdling scream. The player tops the ball and it rolls a few yards down the fairway into a line of trees. Tom is laughing as he goes over to the players. They are laughing, too, with that boyish comradery of athletes that knows no age limit. After a few minutes one of the players hands Tom a driver. He tees up a ball and drives it far down the fairway.

Tom is at ease with his teammates in a way few stars of his magnitude are. He truly likes them all. The rookies, veterans, journeymen, farm boys, city boys, intellectuals, jocks. He is amused, not annoyed, by their natures so different than his. He even likes the Neanderthal Pete Rose, the antithesis of Tom's respectability. Tom told me once that Pete always brought his girlfriends on the team plane, even in front of the other players' wives, who were warned by their husbands never to tell Pete's own wife what they saw on the road.

One night in the clubhouse before a game, Pete came in and regaled his teammates with a story. He was fucking one of his girlfriends on top of a pool table in his basement den when his young son, Pete Jr., came down the stairs and caught his father *in flagrante delicto*. Pete thought that story was hysterical, not humiliating.

"Imagine," Tom said, "that kind of mindset." Yet Tom liked Pete Rose. "He was a good teammate," he said. Tom judges no one, except those players who treat their sport cavalierly. Still, I was afraid he'd judge me and find me wanting. More precisely, I found myself wanting.

While Tom is talking to his teammates on the golf course, I go inside his condo to make a call. The small condo is decorated in an oriental motif. Bamboo chairs. Black oriental chest flecked with gold against a wall. Fine-lined ink drawings of birds on the walls. Laid out across the dining room table are hundreds of tiny puzzle pieces, which, when fit together, will depict a snow-capped Japanese mountain. I try to envision Tom, alone at night, with Nancy and his daughters back in Connecticut, huddled over those pieces, fitting them together painstakingly like a child in kindergarten. Tom, with his infinite patience, trying to distract himself from his loneliness after another poorly pitched game, in the twilight of his career. So he fits each piece into that vast puzzle late into the night to remind himself that each of those pieces was a perfectly thrown pitch in his illustrious career.

I make my call in the kitchen. The woman in my hotel room answers. I say, "I'll be back soon. We'll go to dinner." She says, "How is he?" I say, "The same. Tom never changes." She says, "That's nice." While we talk, I notice a newspaper headline taped on the refrigerator door. It reads: "Seaver Throws Erratic Shut Out At Astros, 4–0." It's precisely the kind of thing Tom would find amusing. I have a quotation from Joan Didion taped above my office desk. It reads: "Writers are always selling someone out."

When I return to the deck, the players are far up the fairway and Tom is talking to his next-door neighbor. A tall, silver-haired man with a farmer's tanned and leathery skin. The man is saying to Tom, "She's been losing weight. I don't know. All we can do is wait for the tests and cry."

"Yeah, well, you gotta cut that out pretty damned quick," Tom says. The old man looks down at his feet. He nods, then walks back to his condo. Tom says to me, "Jeez, it'll break my kids' hearts. She babysits for them. They love her."

I try to change the subject. I tell Tom I like the way he decorated the interior of his condo.

"It was Nancy," he says. "I loved it out here the first moment I saw it. It's peaceful and private. There's nothing but farms around here. I leave on a road trip and the farmers are planting corn. When I get back the corn is waist high. When I first saw these condos there were none available. This was a model, furnished and everything. I said, 'I'll take it.' The real estate guy said, 'You don't understand. It's a model.' I said, 'I don't care. I want it just the way it is, furniture and all.' We bought it and moved in in a day. Jeez, I wished it were that easy with our new house in Greenwich. I was on the road when Nancy saw it. An old barn, but huge. She woke me at five in the morning in my hotel room. 'This is the one,' she said." Tom shrugs. "I was half asleep, but

I knew that house was gonna cost me plenty." He grins at me. "And it did. It needed a ton of work. Bats were living in the rafters. We had to smoke them out."

At 6:00 p.m. I stand up to leave. Tom says, "What's your hurry? Let's go out to dinner. We'll make a night of it. I got nothing else to do."

"I'm exhausted," I tell him. "I got up early and I've been traveling all day. Planes, trains, and automobiles. I'm just gonna get some room service and go to sleep."

"I hear ya," he says. "Been there." He tries not to show me he's disappointed. I try not to show that I'm lying to him. It's not hard to deceive Tom. Tom is not a duplicitous man, like I am.

The following morning, the woman goes home. Late in the afternoon, Tom picks me up outside the hotel and we drive through the city toward Riverfront Stadium in his new BMW 320i. "A nice little car," I say as we wait for a traffic light to change.

"Yeah, it is a nice little car…for seven grand…but it cost sixteen." Then he grins at me and adds, "Actually, I wanted to buy a gold Corvette. With a T-top roof that leaks in the rain. But some asshole bought the last one and he won't sell it."

"Fuck you."

He laughs.

The red light is interminable. Suddenly, Tom leaps out of the car, leaving the door open, and sprints toward a newspaper vending machine on the sidewalk. He searches his pockets for change but has none. So he hands the first person he sees, a young woman, a dollar bill and asks for change. She reaches in her purse, hands him change, and puts his bill in her purse. He smiles and thanks her. She looks at him, stunned. Tom takes the paper from the machine, sprints back to his car, and we drive off. The girl is staring after us.

The ride through rush-hour traffic is stop and go, so to pass the time, as we often do, we rag on each other. We argue about the relative speed of our fastballs, both of which are now past their prime. Mine further past.

"You know, Tom, my fastball is catching up to yours now. What are you throwin', about seventy-eight?"

"Bullshit."

"Remember what Terry Tata said."

"Yeah, and look where it got ya." He points to his windbreaker, on which is written, "Member of the 3000 club." A reference to his career 3,000-plus strikeouts.

I smile at him, a condescending smile, and say calmly, "Yes, Thomas. But remember this: Everyone remembers what Plato wrote. No one remembers who won the Olympic Games when he was writing."

"You're not Plato."

We pull into the Reds parking lot at the stadium. As we walk toward the clubhouse, Tom notices my shoes. Straw Italian loafers. "Who gave you those?" he asks. Then, with mock surprise, he adds, "You *paid* for them?" Tom is wearing penny loafers, baggy chinos, and a polo shirt with an alligator on it.

The Reds clubhouse is filled with players in various states of undress. One, César Cedeño, is walking around naked, his huge cock slapping against his legs. His lean, tightly muscled body is adorned only with gold chains around his neck. I toss César a head fake and say sotto voce to Tom, "A Mr. T starter kit."

Tom glances at César and his swinging dick and raises his eyebrows. "Tells you something about the guy, huh?"

Tom exchanges greetings with his teammates, then introduces me to Joe Nuxhall, a former Reds pitcher, now their TV broadcaster. Joe doubles as the team's batting practice pitcher, although he is about sixty pounds over his playing weight.

Joe shakes my hand. Tom says, "Pat here is a great friend of Steve Garvey."

"Really?" says Joe. "He's a helluva player."

Joe does not get Tom's joke. Steve Garvey and I are not friends. A few years ago, Steve and his wife, Cyndi, sued me and *Inside Sports* magazine for $11.2 million. They did not much like a story I wrote about them. At the time, I told Tom, when I got the lawsuit papers, I was driving my wife's '67 Ford station wagon with body rot. "It was like telling me I was pregnant," I said to Tom.

Tom said, "Why eleven-point-two mil, why not twenty mil?"

I explain Tom's sick sense of humor to Joe. He laughs, then says, "What are you doing here? It sure as hell couldn't be to write about Tom's pitching."

I turn to Tom and say, "I like this guy." All three of us laugh. It's part of what I miss about playing baseball. That sick locker room sense of humor found only among men thrown closely together. Cops, firemen, the military, jocks. Nothing's sacred. So nothing really hurts. In the Real World, when I revert to my jock days and say something sarcastic to a friend who never played sports, they look crushed. I catch myself and say, "No, no! I'm only kidding!"

After Joe moves off, Tom goes over to the clubhouse stereo system with a music tape of a singer he recently discovered. Her name is Alberta Hunter. She is an eighty-seven-year-old black torch singer who began her career in smoky Chicago saloons at the age of twelve. She has only recently been rediscovered, still singing in saloons.

Her scratchy, sexy voice fills the clubhouse. Tom is putting on his long johns at his locker. He sits on a three-legged stool and begins working the *New York Times* crossword puzzle. He looks up and says, "Listen to her. Isn't she great? She quit singing for twenty-four years and just went back to it. She's singing at the Cookery in Greenwich Village." He sticks a wad of chewing tobacco in his mouth and goes back to his puzzle. "What's a four-letter word for an animal that can't reproduce?" He spits tobacco juice into a Styrofoam cup. "Mule," he says, and writes the word.

Alex Treviño, the Reds' catcher, stops by to discuss how Tom will pitch to a certain Houston hitter tonight. "He likes the ball away from him," Treviño says.

Tom, serious now, shakes his head. "No, Alex. I think he likes it inside. He turns his wrists over."

"No. Away, Tom."

Tom shakes his head no. "I don't think so, Alex."

Alex Treviño is twenty-four years old. He has been a starting big-league catcher for three years. Tom Seaver is thirty-eight years old. He has been a starting big-league pitcher for seventeen years. He is firm about what he knows about pitching. But he is also a considerate man. Unlike myself. If I were Tom, I would have snapped at Treviño, "You're a fuckin' kid! You're telling *me* how to pitch?"

After Treviño leaves, Tom says, "You know, I was reading the *Sporting News* the other day and I thought I was leading the league." He grins. "Then I realized I was reading the paper upside down." He goes back to his crossword puzzle. I ask him what is there about crossword puzzles, and the puzzle pieces on his dining room table, that seems to fascinate him.

"It keeps my mind sharp," he says. "Even for pitching. I need total concentration to zero in on the batter, then the pitch. Broadcasting, too." Late in his career now, Tom has talked about having a broadcast career in sports after he stops pitching. "Live broadcasting is tough," he says. "You're under the gun. You have to be organized, get into your story quickly, and get out in thirty seconds. Sometimes taping can be even harder because you know you can blow it and re-tape it, so you don't concentrate as hard. I remember doing a thing for the Special Olympics, you know, retarded kids, and I kept blowing it. It was hot in the sun and I was into my fifth take, and this kid sweating bullets says to me, 'Come on! Get it right!'"

Tom stops talking, cocks an ear to Alberta Hunter singing: "Get your hand off it. It's too delicate for you. I'm saving it. I'm talking about my big red rose." Tom yells out, "She's eighty-seven fucking years old! Do you believe it! She's full of life!" His teammates break into laughter.

At exactly 7:05 p.m.—the game will start in twenty-five minutes—Tom finishes his crossword puzzle and puts on his uniform. "Time to go to work," he says. He leaves the clubhouse. I follow him onto the field toward the warm-up mound halfway down the right-field foul line. While Tom begins to long toss with his catcher, I stand behind him and watch. Tom isn't like most pitchers who assume a threatening demeanor on days they pitch. Steely-eyed stares, like Gary Cooper in *High Noon*, meant to terrorize villains, sportswriters, fans, even their own teammates, from daring to say hello to them, much less ask them a direct question. Steve Carlton, the Phillies' loony southpaw, had a special meditation room built for him off the clubhouse. The room was painted a dark, evening-sky blue, with little stars on the ceiling and an easy chair for Steve to lounge in as he contemplated his pitching strategy for the game while in perfect silence. Just like Michelangelo, in his little meditation room in his Florentine house, contemplating how to reveal the universe of mankind in his masterpieces.

Tom doesn't assume such phony, trancelike personas on days he pitches because he's always himself. So I stand behind him to get a better look at his throwing. It doesn't bother him. Actually, I think he likes it. An audience of one he can talk to.

Without looking back at me, Tom soft tosses with his catcher from ninety feet away. He says to me, "It takes me longer to warm up as I get older. So many parts of my body I have to get warm. Not just my arm."

Finally, he walks to the mound, sixty feet, six inches from his catcher behind a plate. He works quickly now. He catches the return throw from his catcher and begins his motion when the ball hits his glove. When Tom's finally warmed up, the catcher crouches, and

Tom begins throwing his repertoire of pitches. Fastball, slider, sinker, change-up. They're all variations of one pitch, his fastball. The spin on the ball and the speed and movement varies, depending on how he grips the ball, but essentially all four pitches are thrown with a fastball motion. Arm extended straight toward the batter when he releases the ball.

A curveball would require Tom to add a different arm motion to his simple fastball motion. A curveball is the most difficult pitch to throw because it's the only pitch in baseball that requires two arm motions on one pitch. The ball passes the pitcher's head moving toward the batter exactly as would a fastball. But then, when the ball moves in front of the pitcher's head so that he can see it out of the corner of his eye, the pitcher rolls his fingers over the top of the ball while simultaneously pulling his arm down and in toward his left hip. If done properly this creates a fierce downward spin on the ball as it approaches the plate. A few feet from the plate this spin causes the ball to drop straight down, like a hanged man's body falling through a trapdoor. Such curveballs have a name: "the Unfair One."

Tom never had "the Unfair One" because he was a "drop and drive" pitcher. His body was so low to the ground on delivery that it was impossible for him to get his arm up high enough so that he could roll his fingers over the ball and then yank his arm back straight down toward his left hip. That's why, despite his 3,640 career strikeouts, Tom left so many strikeouts on the table. All the great strikeout pitchers, like Sandy Koufax and Nolan Ryan, had devastating overhand curveballs to augment their fastballs. To master that curveball, they threw from a "tall and fall" motion. In mid-delivery, they stood erect, and just as they released their curveball from high over their head, their arm and upper body literally fell straight down off the mound, which generated maximum downward spin on their curveball. It was Ryan's

"Unfair One," not his fastball, that helped him generate most of his 5,714 career strikeouts.

Tom grunts and struggles as he throws fastballs, sinkers, sliders. Pitching never has come easy to Tom. He's a dray horse, not a thoroughbred. Which makes his accomplishments so much more noteworthy.

He does not have his good stuff today and he knows it. It doesn't matter. Often, the stuff he has in the bullpen doesn't resemble his superior stuff in a game. And even if he still has his bullpen mediocre stuff in the game, he'll find ways to adjust to be successful.

Watching Tom throw, I am reminded of myself in the minor leagues. When I didn't have my good stuff, I tried to force it. Throw harder than I was capable of. On the mound, I just got wilder, walking batter after batter. Thinking about it now, I realize that was my way of inventing an excuse for my failure. See? I was wild; they didn't hit my fastball! At all costs, I protected my ego. Not like Tom. His only concern is the result, not his ego.

Tom pitches a strong, if atypical, game for the Tom Seaver I remember with the Mets. Without his strikeout fastball, he gets by with intelligence and doggedness. He gets the Astros to pound his pitches into the ground for six innings before they finally push a run across the plate in the seventh. Tom is tired. When he gets his catcher's return throw after each pitch, he takes more and more time before throwing. He walks around the mound, landscapes dirt with his spikes, stretches his neck, rotates his shoulders, finally throws. He gets out of the inning with a 3–1 lead and he does not return for the eighth. I am waiting for him in the clubhouse before the game is over. I extend my hand, and say, "You did good, Big Guy."

"Thanks," Tom says as we shake hands. He is hyped up, as nervous as any young boy in Little League. Still! After all these years! "I didn't have anything warming up," he says. "But when I got to the mound, I didn't force it. I let it come to me. Like Gil Hodges always said, 'Patience, Tom.'" His uniform is drenched with sweat. He is breathing heavily, his eyes glassy as if he's on drugs, which in a way he is. Adrenaline from a well-pitched game. It is at that moment, for the first time, standing alone with Tom in the Reds clubhouse, that I admire Tom Seaver as much as any man I had ever met.

Tom goes to his locker, strips off his uniform, and sits on his stool in his shorts. He hunches over, still breathing heavily. The trainer comes over and wraps an ice pack around his right shoulder. Tom gets up and goes to the players' lounge. He grabs a beer from the cooler, collapses onto a leather sofa, and makes a call. Nancy picks up on the first ring. They talk. I watch him through an open door from the clubhouse. Tom's head is inclined toward his left shoulder, toward the telephone. He nods as Nancy talks. I hear him ask her about their daughters. She responds. He smiles.

When the game is over and Tom's first victory of the season is assured, his teammates stream into the clubhouse and each, in turn, congratulates him. Then he is surrounded at his locker by newspaper and TV reporters. They ask him questions. He answers, always in the same way, jokingly at first, sarcastic comments about himself, his pitching, and then becomes serious, answering each question thoughtfully in detailed sentences. One of the reporters tells him his fastball was clocked at 88 mph.

"I'm satisfied with that," Tom says.

"You never used to be," a writer says.

Tom does not take the bait. He smiles and says, "Yeah, well, we all get old."

The reporters linger for an hour, until Tom has given them what they need, and then they leave. The clubhouse is almost deserted now. Tom has yet to take a shower. He goes to the stereo and puts on Alberta Hunter's tape. Her scratchy, sexy voice fills the room. Tom stands in the center of the empty room and listens. He cocks his ear to a particular lyric. His face beams. He calls over to me, "Eighty-seven fucking years old! Do you believe it?"

* * *

Tom finishes the '82 season with a 5–13 record and the highest ERA of his career at 5.50. It is the first time in his 17-year career that he has given up more hits, 136, than innings pitched, $111^1/_3$. After that season, the Reds trade him back to the Mets for sentimental reasons. The Mets want Seaver to end his career where he started, and possibly win his three hundredth game with the franchise. It also won't hurt the Mets that when Tom takes the mound at Shea Stadium, he will draw at least twice as many fans as any other pitcher on the team. In '83, Tom's 9–14 record and 3.55 ERA is considerably better than it was when he was pitching for a superior team, the Reds, in '82. He now has only to win 27 games over the next few years in a Mets uniform before he joins that select company of pitchers who have won 300 games in a career.

CHAPTER SIX
1984

I t is late January 1984. The stone walls of the old cellar are cold. Tom has a cold, and yet, dripping sweat, he is throwing baseball after baseball off his new dirt mound into a net. It is his day to throw. He is thirty-nine years old, throwing baseballs into a net in a cold stone cellar in his old barn home in Greenwich, Connecticut. He is coming off a 9–14 season, and a 3.55 ERA, with the Mets in '83, his pitching better than his mere stats. After five superior seasons, and one poor, injury-riddled season in '82, the Reds traded him back to the Mets so Tom could end his career with the team he had started with seventeen years ago. That trade would almost assuredly, barring injury, guarantee that Tom would win his three hundredth career game with the team on which he had once been known as "the Franchise." But it was not to be. The Mets, in their typical ineptitude when it came to Seaver, left him off the protected list during the winter under the assumption no team would pay over a million dollars a year for a thirty-nine-year-old pitcher who had won 14 games and lost 27 the past two years. They were wrong—the White Sox snatched him up on January 20, 1984. And now Tom is preparing for his first spring training with his new team, the Chicago White Sox.

"It's for the best," Tom says. "I'll have a better chance getting to 300 with the White Sox than with the Mets." He picks a ball from a blue bucket, pumps, throws with a grunt, and follows through. The ball hits the net high and bounces back to Tom. He fields it with a swipe of his glove and pantomimes a throw to first base like a young boy pitching an imaginary baseball game in midwinter. "Got him by a step," he says, smiling. Tom is wearing sneakers, baggy blue sweatpants, and a sweatshirt that is too small for him.

"I don't like to start," he says. "It's cold. But once I get warm and can do things with the ball, I love it. Of course, you can't be too fine down here. I just work on mechanics, timing, getting the feel of the ball in your hand. It helps me get ready for spring training. Still, you only have a certain number of pitches in your arm, and I'm using them up down here." He shrugs. "It's a trade-off. It's like having a great bottle of wine in your cellar. You want to save it, but you can only save it for so long before it goes bad."

I tell him what Hemingway said about his writing talent. "It's like a knife blade," I tell Tom. "If you try to save it, it gets dull and rusty. If you use it constantly, it stays sharp, even though it might wear down sooner."

He tilts his head like dogs do when they're confused by their masters. Then he gives me a small smile and says, "You just keep thinking, Butch. That's what you're good at."

"I got vision, Sundance, and the rest of the world wears bifocals."

Tom picks another ball from his blue bucket. Before he can throw it, his small black dog, Penny, curls herself around his legs. Slider is gone. Tom pets Penny with his left hand after taking off his glove. He tries to push her away. "Come on, I can't pet you now. I'm working."

The cellar is musty smelling, low-ceilinged, with weathered and termite-chewed two-hundred-year-old exposed beams, stone walls, and exposed water pipes and electrical wires. There is a pool table and a pinball machine. "I rarely play pool," he says. "I'm not very good so I get bored quickly."

"My father was a card sharp and pool hustler," I say. "He never let me beat him in pool. Maybe I can just beat up on you for a few games. Make me feel good, Tom."

"I would. Give you a little something. But I have no interest. I wouldn't be a worthy opponent."

I point to his exercise cycle, and he says, "I hate pedaling that."

"What about that Cybex leg machine?"

"I hate that, too. Some players get caught up lifting weights to prove how strong they are. They forget what the purpose is: to help them play the game better."

The cellar is the foundation for the huge old barn Tom and Nancy bought a few years ago. It's down the road from their original farmhouse on the golf course. They converted the barren barn, at great expense, into one of those luxurious homes seen in *Architectural Digest*. A builder I know told me of their project, "It would have been cheaper for them to tear down the whole thing and start from scratch." But Tom and Nancy wanted to preserve the antique integrity of the two-century-old three-story barn, so they worked within the confines of the original structure. The result is an open floor plan with huge windows that let in slabs of sunlight even in winter. The floor of the main level, above where Tom is throwing, is covered with foot-square Mexican tiles stained a dull rose color. Tom stained each of those tiles himself. There are green plants everywhere in the great room so that it seems a visitor is both inside a house and outside it at the same time. Like the farmhouse, the barn is sparingly decorated with antique furniture, delicate china in breakfronts, children's toys tossed everywhere, and original, if obscure, oil paintings on the walls.

"The antiques are Nancy's," Tom says to me, between pitches. "The paintings are mine. I don't know much about art, just what I like.

Diebenkorn, a blue-collar California artist." He raises his eyebrows, and smiles, "Like me."

When Tom and Nancy first moved into their converted barn, they shared it with a colony of bats hanging upside down high up in the rafters. "They use to fly down when we ate dinner," Tom says. "Right over the table, with that squeaking sound they make. We couldn't even smoke them out at first." So the Seavers left the house for a few days while the exterminator filled it with smoke. When they returned, the bats were gone, but their house smelled like a barbecue pit for months.

Penny scampers away and Tom goes into his motion, with an imaginary runner on an imaginary first base in the imaginary stadium that is his cellar. He comes to his stretch, pauses, and glances over his left shoulder at the imaginary runner. He says, "They say you get past thirty-five and you lose your velocity. But last year I could still bring it in the nineties when I had to." He glances away from the runner to me and says, "But not like you could bring it, right, Big Guy?" He throws. The ball hits the net low and outside to a right-handed batter. Tom snares the rebound, pantomimes an imaginary throw to his imaginary first baseman.

"If I could have thrown my fastball to that spot," I say, "you'd be interviewing me now."

"Yeah, I threw that ball pretty good. It usually takes me two weeks of throwing in spring training before I can throw that low and outside pitch to righties. First day of throwing, though, I can bust it up and in pretty good. It's getting the ball low and away you have to really bend your back. That gets harder to do when you get older. It's not all about velocity now. There's location and movement of the ball. You can still determine those two. And you learn to change speeds. I've got a great change-up now. Wanna see?" He throws again, and despite his considerable arm speed, the ball moves more slowly toward the screen and seems to fade down and away from a left-handed hitter at the end. "Not bad, eh?" I don't tell him what I'm thinking. How fascinating it is for me to get a tutorial in pitching from such a master, like Hemingway showing me how to cut extraneous words from my sentences, and Faulkner telling me to always be receptive to mystery in my writing.

"I don't have to strike out every batter with my fastball anymore," he says. "I can't. But I can strike out a guy when I need to." He puts his hands on his hips and faces me. "I still wish I had a better curveball. I know! I know! I know! But I'm still trying to understand it, the concept of it. How to make it do what it's supposed to do. It's never too late to learn. My father now, he's seventy, and he still plays golf. He's been in the Pebble Beach Open for thirty-five years. He won it once. This year he teamed with this twenty-four-year-old kid, who tells him, 'Don't worry, I'll read the putts for you.' Imagine!" His voice gets shrill. "Someone so dumb as not to draw on a man's fifty years of experience. That kid'll never learn."

Tom has depleted his bucket of thirty-five balls, some of which he caught, some of which went astray. He goes to the net to pick up the strays. I offer to help. He waves me off. "No, no. I like the bending over for them; good for my follow-through." While Tom bends over for each ball, Penny returns and Tom pets her with his left hand while simultaneously picking up balls and dropping them in the bucket. Then he begins throwing again.

After a quick shower upstairs, Tom, dressed in a plaid flannel shirt, chino slacks, and house slippers, leads me to his office at the far end of the big room. His winter days in Greenwich are always the same. He wakes at six, reads the newspapers, works the *Times* crossword, timing himself on his wristwatch. Tom always tries to finish the latest puzzle in less time than he did the previous one. Then he throws at eleven, or plays squash in town, and then works around the house. "Putters" is a better word than "works." It's what old men do with too much time on their hands. They invent chores for themselves. Tom fusses with his gardens, repairs a stone wall, finishes a wood closet, trims his new wine cellar with oak salvaged from the barn. The oak was gouged and nicked where it had been kicked by the hooves of horses long gone. Tom stripped the wood and refinished it.

"It's beautiful stuff," he says, rubbing his hands sensually over the glistening wood in his office. "Gorgeous. I love it."

Tom sits back in his chair in his office and puts his feet up on his desk, which is cluttered with photographs of his wife and two daughters. He begins flipping through a baseball encyclopedia. When he comes to the stats of Sandy Koufax, the former Dodger left-handed pitcher, he says, "Jeez, he had some great stats." He sounds like every baseball fan in a northern winter for whom baseball is never far from his thoughts even as he looks out the window at the falling snow.

Koufax reached the big leagues right out of high school, at nineteen. His was one of those golden talents, a gift from the gods, as swift as Pegasus, but wild, untamed. Sandy's first six years with the Dodgers, 1955 to 1960, were pretty much a wash as he struggled to control his prodigious natural gifts. He won 36 games, lost 40, struck out his share, but pretty much walked more than his share. When he finally reined in his electric fastball and unhittable overhand curveball, he went on a tear. From 1961 to 1966, Sandy won 129 games, lost only 47, averaged 10 strikeouts, and surrendered only 6.5 hits per game. He won an average of 24 games per season from 1963 until 1966, when, abruptly, at the age of thirty, he retired with an arthritic, sore left arm.

Tom Seaver never had consecutive years of such otherworldly success as Koufax had. Still, he says to me in his office, "I'm satisfied with my career. I've been consistent. That's the kind of thing I admire. I have no disappointments in my career except all that time I've wasted in airports, hotels, and clubhouses. I pass that time reading and playing bridge. Do you know the books of Robert Ludlum?"

I nod. Tom says, "I can read him in the clubhouse. Can you imagine? With all that noise." He smiles. "I just keep turning the pages." He makes the dramatic pause of a bad actor, looks at me with great earnestness, and says, "Maybe you should write books like Robert Ludlum. You'd sell more books."

"Fuck you, Big Guy. And maybe you shoulda learned how to throw a fucking curveball twenty-five years ago. You woulda won a shitload more games."

He laughs, evilly, then says, "Just a suggestion, Big Guy. I'm only trying to help you. Now John Fowles, him I can't read at all. Some of his sentences are a hundred and fifty words long. With big words. I'll bet you love him, don't you?"

"Yep."

"I thought so. Well, I can't read him in the clubhouse. You know how the clubhouse is. One day on the West Coast, we had a day off. I spent it at the Norton Simon Museum looking at paintings. The next day in the clubhouse, one of our old-time coaches asks me what I did on my off day. I told him. He laughed at me and said, 'No, really, Tom, what'd ya do?' I told him again. He said, 'A fucking museum? You gotta be kiddin',' and he walks away shaking his head."

"What did he think you did on your day off?"

"You tell me."

"Yeah."

Tom says, "I could have been playing bridge, too, if I could have found a good game."

"What do you like about bridge?"

"It's a fascinating game."

"Why is it fascinating?"

"It just is."

"But why?"

He looks at me, bemused, and says, "Why? Why? Why? It's always why with you. That's sick. I don't know why. I don't even think about why. I just do it because I like to. Didn't you ever do something just because you liked to?"

"Not until I first figured out why I liked it."

Tom throws up his hands. "I rest my case." He goes back to his baseball encyclopedia. I ask him what he'd like to do with his life now that he's close to retirement. He looks up.

"Manage."

"I thought you wanted to be a pitching coach."

"Nope. I've thought about it. No control. I have to have control."

"What if no one asks you to manage?"

"Then maybe broadcasting. Or maybe I'll just take a year off and travel with the family. We'll go to the Masters and the Kentucky Derby and the Indianapolis Five Hundred. All those things I've never seen. Maybe to Europe, too. I've thought too about going to Georgia to hunt and fish, or maybe just paint the rest of my life. But I don't think painting is realistic. I've got no talent for it."

"You never had any talent for pitching either, but that kinda worked out."

He nods. "That's true. Maybe I could learn how to paint. But I have to do something that's rewarding, a challenge. That's my biggest concern. If I have any fears at all, it's that I won't ever find anything again in my life as challenging as pitching. That would be horrible. But I'm sure I'll find something. It's out there. I just don't know what it is yet."

Tom pauses a moment. Reflecting. Something he doesn't like to do, not because he can't, but because he's avoided reflection for so many years so it wouldn't interfere with his pitching. Now, reflecting on the unknown bothers him. He says, "I guess I shouldn't say 'fear' it. I know I'll find something."

When it's time to leave, Tom walks me to the front door. He takes my coat out of a closet and helps me on with it. Nancy appears, as if on cue. She's smiling her enigmatic smile. She has let her hair, once bleached bright blonde, grow back to its more natural sandy color. She looks more natural than she did years ago when I first met her. But still beautiful. They have both aged well. She comes toward me to shake my hand.

"Was Thomas a good boy today?" she says.

"About usual."

Nancy shakes her head in mock despair. "He wasn't in a very good mood. *People* magazine wants to do a photo layout of us, isn't that right, Thomas? And *People* is not one of Thomas's favorite magazines."

"The last time they sent a photographer to the house," Tom says, "he wanted me and Nancy to pose laying on our bed. This time, he'll probably want us in a hot tub sipping champagne."

Nancy smiles at me. "Better the photographer should shoot Thomas in the shower. With a Stroh's beer in one hand and a cigar stub clenched between his teeth."

I laugh, but Tom shakes his head at this intrusion into his studied privacy. He would not have volunteered to do this story and photo layout if the writer had not been a friend who needed the money.

As I am about to leave, I notice a beautiful, smoothly aged antique breakfront in the hallway. I mention it to Nancy. She laughs, cocks a hip, and pats her behind.

"It is smooth and well rounded," she says. "Isn't it, Thomas? Thomas loves smooth, well-rounded things. Don't you, Thomas?" He looks mortified. Nancy smiles at him. Finally, he smiles, too. She goes over to him and offers up the side of her face to be kissed.

CHAPTER SEVEN

1985

On Sunday, August 4, at Yankee Stadium, Tom Seaver won his three hundredth major league game, 4–1, pitching for the Chicago White Sox. Before 54,032 fans, Seaver pitched a six-hit complete game recording seven strikeouts at the age of forty. It was his twelfth win against eight losses that season. Yet, a year and a half before his three hundredth victory, and before he signed with the White Sox, Seaver, in a rage, threatened to retire from baseball.

● ● ●

In January 1984, Seaver was at a sporting goods convention in Chicago, picking up some loose change signing autographs for fans. In a month he expected to go to spring training with the Mets. Three White Sox executives—the team's owners, Eddie Einhorn and Jerry Reinsdorf, and Roland Hemond, the team's general manager and 1983 MLB Executive of the Year—were at the same hotel where Seaver was staying. They, too, were preparing for spring training by perusing the MLB protected players list to see if they might find a hidden gem among players not protected by their team. When Hemond noticed Seaver's name was not on the Mets' protected list, he assumed he'd missed it. He'd worn glasses for years. So he went over the list again, then a third time. Seaver's name was still not there. Hemond was excited. He considered Seaver not only the best pitcher now available as a free agent, but also a "class guy."

Hemond himself was always a "class guy," and one of the most astute minds in baseball. When I pitched in the Braves system at Davenport in the Midwest League in 1960, Hemond was the Braves' assistant farm director. During the season he traveled around the Braves system evaluating young talent. One night when I was pitching in Keokuk, Iowa, Hemond was in the stands. I had one of my typical games, all promise and despair. In four innings I gave up four runs on two hits and six walks. I also struck out nine batters. After the game, as was my custom, I walked the streets of Keokuk late into the night replaying every pitch, every walk, every strikeout in my mind, trying so desperately to make sense of my pitching. What was I missing? It was like being trapped in a room without light, searching desperately for a lost key in the darkness. All I had to do was find that single key and the door to my pitching success would open up to the sunlight of a beautiful new day. But I couldn't find it.

A car pulled up alongside of me and the passenger-side window rolled down.

A voice called out to me, "Pat! Pat! Come over here." I went to the car window to see Roland Hemond leaning across the seat toward me. He was a nondescript little man, with eyeglasses, who resembled more a high school physics teacher than a great baseball mind. He was smiling at me, an anxious smile. He said, "Don't you worry about it, Pat. You'll get it right. You've got electric stuff. You're gonna be in the Bigs one day soon, son." And then he was gone.

It was one of the few times in his life, Roland Hemond was wrong about a player.

Twenty-three years later, Hemond was one of the three White Sox executives who took turns calling Seaver's Atlanta hotel room a number of times, getting no answer. Finally, late at night, Seaver answered the phone. They told him they'd like to talk to him, but they avoided telling him why. They realized Seaver had no clue he hadn't been protected by the Mets. They had to inform him face-to-face, as delicately as possible. Seaver was less than responsive, but still he invited them to his room. When they broke the news that the Mets had left him off their protected list and the White Sox had chosen him, Seaver was furious. Not at the Sox, but at the Mets, who once again had mishandled his career. Seaver told the executives that he was fed up, and he might as well just retire from the game.

The three men tried to calm him down. They gave him three reasons why he should sign with the Sox. They had a terrific club, and, with Seaver pitching, they had a good chance to go to the World Series. Secondly, they told him he would almost assuredly win his three hundredth game with the Sox since he only needed 27 wins to do so. And finally, for the first time in Seaver's career, they told him he'd become a million-dollar-a-year pitcher. They offered him a one-year contract for $1,131,357. Then Hemond told him that he felt Tom still had the good stuff to maintain his career of excellence. (This time Hemond was right, as he usually was about baseball talent.) So Seaver signed. (After he went 15–11 in his first year with the Sox, they paid him $1,136,262 in his second year, 1985, and $1,132,652 in his third year. Those three contracts almost equaled the amount of money Seaver had been paid for all seventeen previous yearly contracts.)

⬟ ⬟ ⬟

Marty Appel was a Yankees media executive on the day of Seaver's three hundredth win. He told the Yankees WPIX-TV producer that "Tom Seaver's going to win his three hundredth game at Yankee Stadium. It's a sure thing. We should bring in the Mets TV broadcaster, Lindsey Nelson, to call Tom's three hundredth win. I know it'll bring a lot of Mets fans to the stadium."

Seaver started that game no longer the pitcher Mets fans had seen when he'd left the team in '77 during the Midnight Massacre. Tim McCarver, a twenty-year major league catcher, who'd often batted against Seaver at his best, said that when Seaver had his great fastball, "He just threw you fastballs to see if you could hit it. If you fouled a few balls off and had two strikes on you, there was no question of guessing on the next pitch. He'd finish you off with a rising fastball up and in. Tom threw the hardest pitch I ever caught, when I caught him in the 1967 All-Star Game."

Buck Showalter, a major league manager for twenty years, described Seaver's youthful fastball as "a come-again fastball. It exploded with a little hop and come-again action at the end. People don't remember, but MLB used a different radar gun when Tom was pitching. It measured the speed of his fastball as it crossed the plate. Years later they switched to a radar gun that measured the speed of the ball as it left the pitcher's hand. When a pitcher today throws a radar-gun ninety-eight-mph fastball, it crosses the plate at maybe eighty-eight mph. Tom's ninety-eight-mph fastball crossed the plate at ninety-eight mph. When Tom lost that fastball, he still kept throwing it. He just kept it away from the sweet part of the hitter's bat now."

McCarver said, "I never remembered Tom throwing a slider. And he never had a very good curveball, like Nolan Ryan. But when Tom got older, he learned from Ryan how to cut the ball. Ryan learned that from Mike Scott when he went to Houston. Hitters always complained to umpires Ryan was cutting the ball. By the time Tom got to the White Sox, he'd lost miles per hour off his fastball. But he was still the same pitcher he had been. He was always the same pitcher even after he lost that great fastball…. Why not? What'd you expect him to do? That's the only kind of pitcher Tom Seaver could be. Fastball up and in."

In the third inning of his three hundredth win, Seaver gave up a run to the Yankees on two singles. After that, he coasted through the Yankee batting order, working on a four-hitter, all singles. He retired the side in order in the fifth, sixth, and seventh innings, mostly on fly balls hit off high fastballs. He was facing an impressive crew of hitters: Ken Griffey, Don Mattingly, Dave Winfield, Rickey Henderson, Willie Randolph, and Don Baylor. Together, they would appear in thirty-eight All-Star Games, and two would be elected to the Hall of Fame, Henderson and Winfield.

Seaver took the mound in the bottom of the eighth inning with a 4–1 lead. The White Sox had scored all four runs in the sixth inning. They would have scored even more runs if Rudy Law hadn't been tagged out at the plate in a controversial call that ended the inning. Tony La Russa, the Sox's bright young manager, charged the home plate umpire, yelling at him that he never saw the play because he was blocked from view. The umpire tried to ignore La Russa, but La Russa stalked him. When La Russa chest-bumped the umpire, the ump ejected him from the game.

"I was ejected because I was so excited for Tom," said La Russa. "We were all pulling so hard for him. I respected him so much. He wasn't just a veteran hanging on for a check. He still had that passion for the game. He was so smart. An artist. He was never surprised by a situation. I have as much admiration and respect for Tom as I do anyone."

Bob Meacham, the first Yankee batter in the eighth, singled off of Seaver. Then Seaver fanned Henderson and got Griffey to hit a ground ball that forced out Meacham at second. Two outs, Griffey at first, Mattingly at bat. Seaver was taking a lot of time on the mound, as if to catch a breath.

"It was a hot summer day," said La Russa. "Duncan [Dave Duncan, the Sox pitching coach] told me he thought Tom was worn out. I told him that Tom could always get you those last six outs."

Mattingly singled off Seaver, sending Griffey to third. Winfield at bat. Two outs. Duncan to the mound. He was joined by the Sox's pugnacious future Hall of Fame catcher, Carlton Fisk. Duncan believed that the manager and pitching coach should determine whether the pitcher stays or goes. "I agreed with Dave," said La Russa. "Except if that pitcher is Tom Seaver. Then you went with what he told you."

But Duncan had already made up his mind. He said to Seaver, "Thanks, Tom. You gave us all you got." Duncan reached out his hand for the ball. But before he could signal for Seaver's relief pitcher, Fisk snapped, "That's bullshit, Dave! Tom, you can't leave this game. You're Tom Fucking Seaver; you've gotta finish this game." Seaver nodded, told Duncan that he still had enough to get Winfield and finish out the game. Duncan walked off the mound. Seaver and Fisk spoke for a moment at the mound, then Fisk walked back behind home plate as Dave Winfield stepped up to hit. Fisk crouched down and extended his fingers between his thighs. Seaver nodded.

Seaver worked Winfield into a 3–2 count. Then he stepped off the mound and made Winfield wait for the deciding pitch. Seaver knew Winfield was a "spotlight" hitter who liked to get the big hit in a clutch situation in front of a big crowd. So Seaver made him wait, Winfield getting anxious to get a swing at Seaver's now faded fastball. Finally, Seaver stepped back on the rubber, went into his motion, and struck out Winfield on a change-up to end the inning.

⬟   ⬟   ⬟

Tom finished the 1985 season with a 16–11 record, 3.17 ERA, and 304 career victories. The Sox quickly re-signed Tom to another $1 million-plus, one-year contract for '86. Tom started off that season pitching poorly and after 12 starts was saddled with a 2–6 record and 4.38 ERA. The White Sox began to shop him around to other teams for a trade. They went first to the Mets, assuming they might want to sign Tom for his last season and milk his signing for all the PR they could to put fans in the seats. Mets GM Frank Cashen was interested, but his manager, Davey Johnson, wasn't. Johnson felt that the return of Seaver to the Mets for one last go-round would create a circus atmosphere, and he wouldn't be the ringmaster. So he nixed the trade. Finally, the White Sox convinced the Red Sox to assume the bulk of Tom's heavy salary for the rest of the '86 season.

Tom became a much-improved pitcher with the Red Sox, finishing with a 5–7 record and 3.80 ERA before a leg injury sidelined him for the year, and the playoffs. Dan Shaughnessy, a sports columnist for the *Boston Globe*, describes all of Seaver's 16 starts as "quality starts. If he didn't get hurt, the Bosox would have won the World Series [against the Mets]."

Richie Gedman, Boston's young All-Star catcher, caught Seaver's last major league victory, his 311th, on August 18, just before Seaver injured his leg. "By then," Gedman says, "Tom was pitching on his knowledge. A lot of hitters thought they were hitting against the Tom Seaver of old, and he took advantage of that. He expanded hitters' zones so they'd get themselves out. If he didn't get hitters to chase a fastball off the plate, then he came inside on them. I remember one game he struck out Cleveland's Cory Snyder three times on eighty-seven-mph fastballs at his neck. After the last strikeout, Cory told me, 'That was the fastest pitch I ever saw.' He wasn't chasing Tom's fastball as much as he was chasing the illusion of the Tom Seaver of old. What was really cool was when Tom faced Reggie Jackson. It was baseball theater. The Shoot-Out at the OK Corral. Strikeout or home run. Reggie always had trouble with the high fastball, so Tom just kept throwing them as if defying Reggie to hit one."

Tom Seaver was fortunate during his career to pitch to two of the best catchers in baseball during that time, Gedman and Jerry Grote of the Mets, and two of the greatest catchers in the history of baseball, Johnny Bench and Carlton Fisk. Seaver wasn't much like the youthful Gedman, nor the sour Grote, nor the cheerfully dim Bench. But no two men in sport were more alike than Seaver and Fisk in so many ways, as men and baseball players. And yet they were dissimilar, too, in one or two profound ways.

During the winter of '86–'87, the Bosox offered Seaver a $500,000 contract for '87. Tom demurred. He said it wasn't enough, and talked of retirement. Then, again, the Mets came sniffing around. They offered him a conditional tryout early in the '87 season. Dennis D'Agostino, a twenty-six-year-old Mets media executive at the time, says, "Although Tom was always in uniform, he wasn't a member of the team then. He hadn't signed a contract yet." D'Agostino was essentially assigned as Seaver's valet, to fulfill any of his wishes, such as finding and returning his charcoal sketch pad Tom had misplaced. "I was so intimidated by him," he says. "He never said three words to me. You had to earn your spurs with Tom. I earned mine when I found that sketch pad."

In June of '87, Tom Seaver pitched in two minor league exhibition games. D'Agostino remembers that in one of those games, "Barry Lyons, a backup minor league catcher, hit two home-run bombs off him. After the game, I walked past Tom's locker. He was sitting there with his back to me. The next day he announced his retirement. After that we always referred to Barry Lyons as an All-Star catcher."

On the day of his retirement, Tom Seaver said that he quit because he had used up all the competitive pitches in his arm.

Photo courtesy of Connecticut Post/Hearst Connecticut Media

12-Year-Old Pat Jordan Has Hurled
Four Straight No-Hit Ball Games

Stratfield Little Leaguer Also Boasts of Six Shutouts

By JOHN JOHANSEN

He's a bit too young yet to command the attention of major league scouts, but 12-year-old Patric Jordan, who pitches for the Stratfield team in the Fairfield Little League, already has made a good start on the road to baseball fame.

The talented right-hander hurled his fourth consecutive no-hit, no-run game Thursday night and in so doing, ran his string of shutouts to six in as many starts this season. He has also twirled two one-hitters and racked up a total of 96 strikeouts in 36 innings, which is pretty fair pitching in any league.

Leads League in Homers

In addition to his skill on the mound, Pat has proved himself to be a good hitter and leads the league in home runs with a total of four. He is the son of Mr. and Mrs. Patrick M. Jordan, who reside at 1134 Valley road, Fairfield, and attends Lincoln school.

The Stratfield team, sponsored by Smirnoff's Super-Market, is coached by Ben Diamond and his assistant, Curt Helgren. Other teams entered in the National division of the Fairfield Little League are the Fairfield Townies, Gould Manor and Labbance.

Two of Pat's no-hitters were twirled against the Townies as the Stratfield lads won by 6-0 and 15-0 scores. He also accomplished the feat at the expense of the Labbance and Gould Manor teams in gaining respective 5-0 and 17-0 victories.

The Stratfield star's 1952 record was not as impressive, but he performed with the Fairfield All-Star team in the District championship tournament and came through with a brilliant bit of relief pitching by striking out the side in the late innings of a close game.

Little League in Fairfield, CT.
Me in mid-motion with my
high leg kick.

I'd just graduated high school and turned eighteen when this photo was taken at the Braves Milwaukee County Stadium in 1959. I am in the center, looking to my left at Warren Spahn, the greatest left-handed pitcher ever. He took a liking to me. To my right is Whitlow Wyatt, Braves pitching coach.

Me in wind-up for the Fairfield Prep High School team before I signed
with the Braves. 1959.

My second year with the Braves in the Florida winter league in Bradenton, FL. I am tagging out Ty Cline, Cleveland Indians outfielder, at home plate. 1960.

Photo by Kelley L Cox – USA Today Sports

Tom and I deep in conversation about the nuances of pitching at a café in Calistoga, California, home of his vineyards, in 2013.

Tom in his vineyard office at his home on a mountain top in Calistoga, California. Tom is laughing at something I said, which somehow always made him laugh.

Tom and I in his vineyards with Tom explaining something to me about growing grapes which I tried, but failed, to express interest in.

CHAPTER EIGHT

2013

PART I

I am standing on the sidewalk in front of the deli when the truck parks at the curb. It's early morning, sunny, cool, a dry Napa Valley day. Good for growing grapes. The Ford F-250 is caked with dirt. A workingman's truck, a vineyard worker's truck. The big guy who gets out is wearing a trucker's cap, flannel shirt, dirty jeans, work boots, and a pair of grape-pruning shears on his belt. He looks over the truck's bed at me. I laugh. He says, "What's so funny?" I say, "You still look like Tom Seaver." He has streaks of silver in his sandy-colored hair, a craggy yet still boyish face, and that high-pitched, girlish voice I remembered.

Tom and I have known each other for forty years. We used to see each other once in a while in our thirties, play one-on-one basketball games at the Greenwich, Connecticut, YMCA, meet at the Mets' stadium when he was pitching, at spring training in Florida, then later in Cincinnati after the Midnight Massacre. In our forties and fifties, after Tom had retired, we'd bump into each other at Mets or Yankees games, where I was working on a story and Tom was broadcasting games on TV. He had gotten fat by then. A fat TV guy wearing garish aqua-blue sports jackets and yellow ties around a shirt collar too tight for him. I no longer wrote many sports stories for magazines by then. In the '90s I was writing novels, crime stories for *Playboy*, celebrity profiles for *GQ*, and long profiles of writers, theater and film actors, and directors for the *New York Times Sunday Magazine*. Tom and I rarely talked over the phone anymore. What was there to talk about? My profile of Mickey Rourke for the *Times Magazine*? His broadcast of a Mets game against the Phillies on a Tuesday night? My advice to him on how to throw a curveball? Or maybe just to remind him that I had a superior fastball? So long ago I could barely remember if that was true or not. Then, in the early 2000s, my estranged daughter called to tell me my grandson I'd never met would like me to get him a baseball players' autograph. So I called Tom, and our relationship resumed again, two reclusive old guys in our seventies now, still trying to one-up each other, but no longer on the basketball court.

He and Nancy had moved to a mountaintop in Calistoga, California, with their three dogs, and Susan and I had moved to an isolated little hill town in the western upstate of South Carolina with our four dogs. We were all, in our old age, seeking the same thing, I guess. Peace and seclusion.

Tom walks around the truck in that slump-shouldered, graceless plowman's walk that he's always had, even when he was a young pitcher with the Mets. He plodded to the mound as if to a hated back-breaking job. As if *he* was the dray horse who had to plow the fields. He was always a blue-collar pitcher, a dray horse, never a thoroughbred. He wasn't born "Tom Seaver, the Franchise," with a blinding God-given talent. He made himself into "Tom Seaver" through a monumental act of will, discipline, intelligence, and hard work.

We shake hands. He says, "You got old."

"No shit. Tell me something I don't know."

"Your beard is white."

"You forget I'm older than you, Tom."

"That's a fact."

"And smarter, too."

He hangs his head like a boy and says, "Aw, I don't know about that."

We sit at a table in the deli and order breakfast. Tom spreads a newspaper on the table and, hunched over, studies it through his reading glasses, like Bob Cratchit at his accountant's desk, studying figures for Scrooge. When he was a famous pitcher in his youth, he opened the newspaper every morning and studied the previous night's box scores. Today he studies the weather to check on his "babies."

When I called him a few weeks ago, very early in the morning, he answered out of breath. I said, "It's me."

He said, "I know."

"What are you doing?"

"I was sleeping until *you* woke me up."

"Oh, Jeez, Tom, I'm sorry. I forgot the time difference."

I heard his evil cackle, and then he said, "I been up two hours, watching the sun rise."

"You prick!" He laughed. "You're out of breath watching the fucking sun rise?"

"I was working, Big Guy, taking care of my babies."

"Your grandkids are there?"

"No, my babies. My grapes."

"Tom, you gotta get a life."

"Like yours? Sitting in an empty room, staring at a blank piece of paper in a typewriter every day for hours."

"I write on a computer now."

"Same thing."

He was right, of course. My life hadn't changed since 1963. The same thing every day. Up at 5:00 a.m. Coffee, the newspapers, the gym, and then sitting at my desk for five hours. But he had a new life now, Tom Seaver, owner of the Seaver Vineyards on Diamond Mountain, Calistoga, California. Which was why I called him in the first place. To reconnect. I said, "We're both old men now, Thomas. Who knows how much longer we've got." He agreed. So, I spent sixteen hours driving, waiting in airports, flying, changing planes, driving some more just to see Tom Seaver again. The greatest right-handed pitcher of the modern baseball era. A twelve-time All-Star, three-time Cy Young Award winner, 311-game winner, a career 2.86 ERA, over 3,000 strikeouts, and the recipient of the highest-ever percentage of votes, 98.84%, of any Hall of Fame member at the time. And, as always, my idol, as, I am sure, I am his.

When he finally turns to the sports pages to check out the Tiger-Red Sox score in the American League Championship Series, he throws up his hands, knocking off his cap, and grabs his hair like a frustrated, emotional teenager, which, in ways, he always was and still is. The Tigers' pitcher, Max Scherzer, had pitched brilliantly for seven innings, beating the Bosox 5–1 on a two-hitter, until he was yanked in the eighth inning. His relief pitchers gave up five runs in the next three innings, including David Ortiz's grand-slam home run, for a 6–5, ten-inning Red Sox win.

Tom screeches like a girl, "Why'd they take Scherzer out?" I say because he'd reached his 109-pitch count. He screeches again, "Pitch count? Pitch count? Baseball's not brain surgery. You don't look for a reason to take him out. You look for a reason to leave him in! Guys like him and Verlander, their three set-up men and closer don't equal them or else they'd be starting pitchers! I'll tell ya, you wouldn't be able to get Bob Gibson off the mound in the eighth inning." Then he tells me a story. Actually, three stories, all linked by a common thread.

When Tom was pitching for the White Sox, as he was approaching his three hundredth win, he was warming up in the bullpen before a game. Dave Duncan, the pitching coach, watched him throw. He shook his head and said, "Tom, you don't have shit." Tom said, "Yeah, so what?" Tom pointed to the other team's dugout and said, "They don't know that! So what's the problem? By the time they find out, it'll be too late."

In his younger years, when his legs were stronger, Tom was famous for driving so hard off the mound and low to the ground that he always scraped his right knee in the dirt. On this day, in his fortieth year, after he finished his warm-ups, the knee of his right pants leg was still white. He reached down with one hand, scooped up some red dirt, and rubbed it over his right knee.

He said to Duncan, "Let them think I still got it."

A few games later, when he was on the mound in the eighth inning with runners on base, Ozzie Guillén, his young, excitable shortstop, came to the mound. Tom says to me now, "Ozzie was like a baby robin, always chirping. He thought I was in trouble. He said, 'Hey, Tom. Dun worry, mon. I get you outta thees. Jess make 'em heet to me.' So I said to him, 'OK, Ozzie, where do you want me to make them hit it, to your left or your right?' He looked at me and said, 'You serious, mon?' I said, 'Absolutely.' Ozzie's eyes got big and he said, 'Mon, you crazy.' I said, 'Now Ozzie, that's an entirely different issue.'"

I laugh out loud. Tom reaches his hand across the table and taps his fingers on my arm. "Serious," he says. "I wasn't kidding. If I executed correctly, I could do that." Then he tells me a third story.

Story three took place during his earlier years with the Mets. Again, he was pitching in the later innings with runners on base. Before the catcher threw the ball back to him, Tom crouched like a quarterback in the huddle, propped his elbows on his knees, and stared at the dirt. His pitching coach, Rube Walker, came hustling out to the mound. Rube said, "Tom, Tom, you all right? You hurt? Maybe you should come out." Tom looked up at him as if he had no idea why Rube was there. He said, "What the hell you doing here? This is my mound, get the fuck off it." Rube said, "But Gil [Hodges] thought you might be in trouble." Tom said, "Trouble? I was fucking thinking. Now get the fuck out of here."

Tom was known for chasing off the mound his pitching coaches and managers, even Yogi Berra and Tony La Russa, with the same words: "Get the fuck off my mound. You got nothing to tell me I don't know." Tom was a throwback to the days when pitchers finished what they started. It's part of his workingman's ethos. You don't leave the construction site because you're tired! You put in a full day's work for a full day's pay. Tom signed on for 647 games as a starter and finished 231 of them. He pitched until he couldn't get anyone else out, and only then did he come out of the game, usually against his will.

"There was no pitch count in those days," Tom says to me. "I regularly threw a hundred thirty-five pitches or more. It's what I was capable of. There should be different rules for different pitchers."

I mention Justin Verlander, whom I knew. "He's a horse," I say.

Tom says, "Then he should have different rules for him." Tom believes young pitchers today hurt their arms, not because they throw too many pitches in a game, but too few. Pitchers strengthen their arms by throwing.

"Like Hemingway said about his writing talent," I say. "It's like a knife. You gotta use it to keep it sharp."

"Absolutely," Tom says. "Look at Joba Chamberlain and Stephen Strasburg. They were babied and still hurt their arms." He explains that pitchers hurt their arms for many different reasons. An accident, like slipping off a muddy mound, genetics, bad throwing mechanics. Who's to know why a pitcher hurts his arm? A mystery. But in today's game there's no room for mystery, only numbers, statistics. So Scherzer comes out after 109 pitches, the Tigers lose the game and the playoffs, and Jim Leyland, their manager, retires. Possibly from embarrassment for making a decision he now knows he shouldn't have made.

The waiter brings our food. A bran muffin and orange juice for Tom, pancakes for me. Tom takes a plastic baggy out of his shirt pocket and empties a bunch of pills on the table. He begins popping one after another into his mouth. "Mostly vitamins," he says. "I have stage three Lyme disease from a deer tick back in Connecticut years ago. It was dormant for years until a few months ago. I thought my mind was going. I couldn't remember things." He says he thought he was suffering the onset of dementia. He became fearful, withdrawn, for the first time in his life. He was afraid he'd get lost in the New York City streets he used to own. It was almost a relief for him to find out, after some tests, that he had Lyme disease, which could be controlled by vitamins, medicine, diet, but no wine, a cruel irony. And mental stimulation. That's another reason why I was there.

When I called Tom to tell him when I'd arrive, Nancy answered the phone. She said, "I'll make a note for Tom to make sure he remembers." Then, after a pause, she told me about Tom's Lyme disease. "He forgets things," she said. "He hasn't done anything like this in years. We talked about it and we decided it's time." Then after a pause, she said, "I'm glad you're coming, Pat. It will be good for Tom. Someone to talk to. Someone to stimulate him." "Stimulate" was not quite the right word to describe what Tom and I did for each other. "Aggravate" was a better word, or as Tom used to put it, I would drive him mad with my incessant intellectually abstract questions.

"Tom, did you ever think about innocence?" I once asked. He looked at me. "I mean, if you lose it, can you ever get it back?"

"Who thinks about such shit?" he said. "Innocence! You either have it or you don't."

Ever since I left baseball, I've spent my life thinking about such "shit." Innocence. Guilt. Anger. Despair. My failure as a pitcher. As a man. All that "an unexamined life is not worth living" shit wears a man down, is detrimental to a happy life. But still necessary to live a life, the right kind of life. Tom doesn't think about such things because they are not as significant a part of his life as they are mine. He has spent his life thinking about and doing what makes him happy. Physical work, pitching, gardening, sweating, his hands caked with dirt. It's how we're different. Oscar and Felix. Except in some ways, we're not different. I'm a blue-collar guy, too, who just happens to be doing a white-collar job. Tom's a blue-collar guy who hid his very considerable intellect as if embarrassed by it.

"My brain is almost working again," he says as he swallows the last of his pills. "But I still have short-term memory loss."

"Me, too. We're getting old, Tom."

He shrugs, says, "Maybe. Lyme disease makes me sleep a lot, too. I was tired all the time." Then he smiles. "But yesterday I worked twelve hours in the vineyard. That was a great day."

I tell him I never sleep. Two hours, then awake three hours, lying in bed, staring at the ceiling, counting my sins leaping over a fence like black sheep. When I told that same story to an Irish editor of mine, a homely, red-faced man, an alcoholic, a homosexual, a Roman Catholic, God forbid, he said, "Ah, Paddy me boy, not to worry. It's not how you run the race that counts, it's how you end it that counts."

Tom says, "That's 'cause your brain is always working. You have to get it right." He adds, "You want to sleep? Get Lyme disease." Then he tells me another story.

When his daughter Sarah was seventeen, she was diagnosed with Hodgkin's disease. "The doctor told her she'd never have children because of the radiation," Tom says. His eyes redden with tears, but then his anger stops the tears. He says, "I walked out of that doctor's office and I said to myself, 'That doctor doesn't know shit about *my* daughter.'" He calms himself, smiles at me, and says, "She got married and had three sons, boom-boom-boom. I told her, 'Sarah, enough already.' She said, 'Dad, I've never been so happy in my life.'"

We eat in silence for a few moments. Then Tom says, "Did I tell you the Ozzie story?" I say, "Yes, you did." He says, "Oh! I forgot. The Lyme disease. Do you know Ozzie?"

"His wife's gorgeous. Like one of those Venezuelan beauty queens."

"I didn't ask you that."

"But she *is* beautiful!"

"I don't care. Just answer the fucking question."

"I'm just giving you some context. You know, writerly details to flesh out the picture."

He glares at me. "Do. You. Know. Ozzie?"

"Yes."

"Thank you very much."

"You're still a pain in the ass."

He laughs. "I'm supposed to be a pain in the ass...to *you*." He looks at my empty plate. "Didn't you get anything to eat?" I nod. He says, "Oh, right, the...you had...the..."

"Pancakes."

"Right. You gotta fill in the words for me sometimes." I nod, change the subject.

I ask him about his fascination for sticking his hands in dirt. Ever since I'd known him in 1971, in Connecticut, he was an avid gardener. He tells me at the deli that his father used to be in the raisin business in Fresno, but gardening didn't interest Tom until he got to the big leagues. It was a good way to relax between games. "I love the artistry of it," he says. "Laying out the flowers in aesthetic patterns. But never on days I pitched. I was afraid I might hurt my hand." He went from flowers to grapes and a vineyard after he'd been out of baseball for about ten years. It was a natural progression for him, a return to his home state, back to gardening, and a vineyard, because during his baseball career he'd cultivated a taste for fine wine. He once spent $4,000 on wine in a Milwaukee liquor store. Milwaukee?

"Outlining a vineyard is the same as outlining your pitches for a game, or outlining an artwork," he says. "I shouldn't tell you this, 'cause I don't want you to think I didn't value my pitching. But if I could go back and have a second run at it, I'd have become an artist. I would have loved to have been a great artist. I would have quit pitching if I could paint like Monet or Rousseau. But I can't. What I could do is pitch, and I could do that very well."

So now he's just a day laborer in his vineyards. "My vineyard manager is my teacher," he says. "I just do what he tells me. Every day is exciting for me. I get mad when the sun isn't up yet. I'm a single-focus guy. Pitching. The vineyard. I'm the worker. I pick up crap. Trim the vines a little. I did that yesterday for twelve hours; worked all my muscles and slept like a baby."

When Tom first bought his property on the top of Diamond Mountain, he found a place where he could grow zinfandel grapes for his favorite wine. He hired a vineyard manager, Jim Barbour, who told him, "You don't do zin on Diamond Mountain. You do cabernet." Tom grins, says to me, "So I told him, 'That's what I said, Jim. I want to grow grapes for cabernet.' I don't argue with anyone anymore. I'm on a learning curve. I've reversed the role I had when I pitched. Nobody came to the mound and told me what to do. I'd earned my stripes. Now I ask the questions. I'm a big pain in the ass…like you. I do what I'm told now, and it's fascinating for me."

"Too bad you didn't do what I told you forty years ago. I coulda taught you how to throw a curveball."

He looks at me, not the wise guy now, and says, "Maybe I shoulda."

After breakfast we go outside. It's warm now, in the sun. The little town has come alive, the sidewalks crowded with tourists in shorts with backpacks, fanny packs, bottled water. Calistoga is one of those picturesque 1890s Napa Valley towns: old Victorian houses and redbrick buildings renovated into bed-and-breakfast hotels, trendy restaurants, boutiques, wine stores. There was a wine tasting in every third store on Lincoln Avenue, the main drag. Calistoga began as a mining town, silver and mercury, and then became an agricultural area, grapes, prunes, walnuts. When hot springs were discovered there, it became a health-spa destination, and still is. It was briefly a winery town, too, in the late 1800s. But then a vineyard disease ruined the plants and Prohibition came along, then the Great Depression. It wasn't until the late 1930s that the area returned to its vineyard and wine days that it is now famous for.

Tom gets into his truck. I go to the passenger side and look through the open window to tell him I'd follow him to his house in my rental car. The inside of his truck is a mess, vineyard dust coating the interior like a powdery film, Styrofoam coffee cups, tools, papers, crumpled bags littering the seats and the floor. I say, "Jeez, Tom, this looks like the kinda truck a guy drinks out of a paper bag in."

"I told you I don't drink anymore," he says. "Besides, I keep it this way so no one will want to get in it. But I'm thinking of getting a new one. I saw one at a Ford dealership with a row of lights on the roof. I told the salesman, 'That's the one I want, an F-250 with lights on the roof.' The guy said only the F-350 came with the lights." Tom looks at me with that mischievous grin of his and says, "I told him, 'You wanna sell me a truck, put the fucking lights on the 250.'"

I follow him out of Calistoga, ringed with mountains. He turns down a two-lane blacktop with vineyards on either side and mountains beyond. He pulls his truck over, parks on the side of the road, and gets out. I park behind him and get out. "I just wanted to show you," he says, and points to the top of a mountain. "See that tiny little open space at the top?" I nod. "That's where our house is. We can see the whole valley from there."

We stand in the sun, looking up at the mountain for a moment. Then Tom says, "Did I ever tell you the McCovey story? No, I didn't." So he tells me.

Tom used to plan out his game the way an artist sketches out a painting four days before he pitched against a team. He was as methodical as a CPA. Tom Seaver's Rules for Pitching.

"Pitching is simple," he says. "If you dissect pitching seven days to Sunday, you're done." The first pitch of every inning is the most important. That pitch had to be a strike. The first batter of every inning was the most important. He had to get that batter out. He tried never to put the potential winning run on base with a walk or, God forbid, an intentional walk. Once, when pitching for the White Sox, his manager, Tony La Russa, came to the mound and told him to intentionally walk the potential winning runner. Tom refused. He tells me, "Tony always thought too much, until I trained him."

Another rule was, a pitcher should never get beat in a crisis situation with anything but his best pitch. Tom's best pitch was a 98-mph fastball that he could throw wherever he wanted to. And finally, a pitcher must always avoid his WCS. He tells me, "I always tried to avoid my worst-case scenario, and if I couldn't, I had to have a plan on how to deal with it when it came up. This one game against the Giants, you can guess what my WCS was." I say, "Willie McCovey with the bases loaded." He says, "Thank you very much. So what do you think happens in the late innings?" I smile. He says, "Thank you very much. Willie McCovey up with the bases loaded. So I'm saying to myself, 'OK, Big Guy, you think you're so hot, a couple of Cy Youngs, what do you do now?'"

He looks at me as if he was seeing that moment right now, by the side of a road between vineyards in Calistoga, California, thirty years later. Big Willie McCovey waiting at the plate, the bat on his shoulder. Tom says, "This is my all-time favorite moment in baseball. I managed to get a three-two count on Willie, and all of a sudden it came to me. I'm in my stretch and I keep checking the runner on first. Now everyone knows the runner can't go anywhere, the fucking bases are loaded, so what is Seaver doing? I keep checking him, refusing to make eye contact with Willie, throwing him a little birdseed, getting him to think, 'What the fuck is Seaver doing?' I wanted him to be anxious, confused." Tom stops talking.

I blurt out, "So what happened?"

"I struck him out on a change-up. Twenty years later we're at the Hall of Fame and Willie says to me, 'Tom, why the hell did you throw me a change-up in that game?"

"Why did you?" I say. "You broke your own rule."

"That's the point, Big Guy. Everyone knew how methodical I was. How this pitch *had* to be a fastball. I was Tom Seaver. So this time I went on instinct." He looks at me with a grin. "Even Tom Seaver has to acknowledge mystery in life."

A few minutes later, I'm driving behind Tom's truck up Diamond Mountain Road. It's very steep, narrow, and curving, with a dark canopy of trees hanging over it. There's no guardrail, only soft dirt on the side of the road and a steep falloff that tumbles down the mountain. We pass a few mailboxes by the side of the road and driveways that go far back into the woods where houses and vineyards are. Tom pulls his truck off into a driveway, stops at an electronically controlled gate, opens it, and drives through. I follow for a few hundred yards until the driveway dips down a bit and suddenly we're in front of his house, perched on the edge of the mountain.

CHAPTER NINE
2013
PART II

Tom's house on top of a mountain in Calistoga, California, is one of those low, ultramodern homes out of *Architectural Digest*, poured concrete and glass walls everywhere and dun-colored wood that blends into the mountain. We go into the kitchen. Tom introduces me to his other daughter, Anne. The Seaver Vineyards is truly a family-run operation. Anne, Nancy, and Tom's nephew's wife run the business side. Tom does the grunt work. I see Nancy to my left at her desk in the loft, talking on the phone. Tom says, "Nancy's in charge of the business side. I can't concentrate on that stuff 'cause of the Lyme disease. Besides, I hate sitting at a desk."

Anne lowers her voice and says, "Dad, Mom's so smart when it comes to business."

"Yeah, she always had this thing about not going to college. This is good for her." Tom and Nancy have been married for over forty-seven years. Tom tells me that the secret was, "Nancy accepted [that] we didn't live a normal life. I could tell her what I did at the office [on the mound] if I had a good day, and if I didn't have a good day, she knew I wasn't talking to anybody. She accepted it." Today, with Tom's short-term memory loss, Nancy watches over him. She leaves Post-its all over the house to remind him of things, like meeting me for breakfast this morning. A longtime friend of Tom's once told me, "Nancy's always been the power behind the throne."

Anne excuses herself and goes upstairs to help her mother. Tom gives me a tour of the house with its poured concrete floors and wide-open spaces, one room flowing into another, only a few of the rooms separated by interior walls.

I notice a crack in the concrete floor. While I'm debating with myself whether to mention it to Tom, he says, "That's the way it came out, so we left it." I remember what he had told me years ago about imperfections. That he didn't have to have everything in his life perfect, like the paneling around the wine flues in his basement, because it would exhaust him, always striving for perfection. Except for his pitching. *That* he had to make perfect.

Tom points to an Andy Warhol painting on the wall of himself as a young pitcher. It's just a photograph, surrounded by a few colorful splashes of paint. He points to two smaller paintings on the inside of an exterior wall. They are identical paintings of an ace of spades from a deck of cards, except that one ace is red and the other is black.

"Richard Diebenkorn," Tom says. "My favorite artist. I wish I could paint like him." Diebenkorn was a Northern California painter, mostly modernist in style, although he also experimented with realism and impressionism. He had a reputation for being a blue-collar, hardworking artist without pretensions.

We go into Tom's small office. It looks unused, as if Tom rarely sat behind his desk. But it's still perfectly decorated with baseball memorabilia, photos of himself, teammates, other famous players, his parents, his daughters. There are books on shelves, a few of them mine, some of which I sent him, some Tom must have bought himself. I wonder if he read them. If he did, he never told me what he thought of them. Tom never did ask me about myself. What I was writing, how I was feeling, my life. Our conversations were always about him, his pitching, his contracts, his life. When I told this to one of Tom's oldest friends, the friend said, "I can get on board with that."

There's an entire wall of mostly old and scuffed baseballs from his achievements, the letters and numbers written on them so faded as to be almost illegible. He shows me a copy of Hank Aaron's autobiography, inscribed by Hank to Tom.

"My favorite player," Tom said.

"Why? He's not a pitcher."

"I wasn't just a pitcher. I was a baseball fan. These guys were my heroes. I love the history of the game." He shakes his head with disgust. "Guys today don't care about the game's history." Then he remembers something, that I had signed with the Braves in 1959. He says, "Did you know Hank?"

I said, "Yes. I went to spring training with him in 1960. I pitched against him in an intra-squad game."

"How'd you do?"

"Walked him on four pitches. The story of my career." Tom laughs. Then I remembered a Hank Aaron-Tom Seaver story Tom had told me years ago. In Tom's first season with the Mets, at twenty-three, he made the National League All-Star team. Before the All-Star Game, he told me he approached Hank in the dugout and said, "You don't know me, Mr. Aaron, but I'm a fan of yours. Could you autograph this ball for me?" Aaron said, "I know who you are, kid. And pretty soon every baseball fan will know who you are." Years later, after Hank retired, a reporter asked him who was the toughest pitcher to hit he ever faced. Hank said, "Tom Seaver."

Tom says, "I was a Braves fan when I was a kid. I loved their uniforms."

"It was navy pinstripes for me," I say. "But that didn't work out." Then I remembered something. "I knew Roland Hemond, too," I say. "The guy who signed you for the White Sox. He was the Braves' assistant farm director when I signed. A great guy." I hesitate a moment, debating with myself, then I say, "He was always kind to me." I told Tom about that night in the Midwest League in 1961 when I struck out and walked so many batters I only lasted four innings in the game. "Must have thrown a hundred pitches," I say. Tom laughs. Then I tell him what Hemond said to me when he pulled his car over to the sidewalk at midnight where I was walking, depressed out of my mind. I say to Tom, "He told me not to worry. He said I had electric stuff and I'd be a big leaguer soon."

"Yeah," Tom says. "How'd that work out for you?" I knew I shouldn't have told him that story. But as usual, I couldn't stop myself.

Tom shows me some of his cherished baseballs on aluminum racks that run up an entire wall. A scuffed Babe Ruth League ball. The ball he threw for the last out of his three hundredth win, and another ball he used for his twentieth victory, the first year he ever won twenty games. His prized possession, though, is a scuffed Little League ball from 1957. He holds it up for me and says, "I pitched a perfect game."

I say, still pissed off at him, "Really? I pitched four consecutive perfect games in Little League and struck out every batter I faced except two."

"Yeah, well, you gotta move on, big boy."

He's right, of course. I never bring up my baseball past with anyone but Tom. It's a childlike obsession, an irrational compulsion to let him know that I pitched, too. I'd even sent him a photograph taken of me in a Milwaukee Braves uniform at County Stadium in 1959. I was on the field, standing between the Braves' pitching coach, Whitlow Wyatt, and Warren Spahn. Spahnie and I were smiling at each other, teammates, me with my amused smile. I was eighteen. The same age Tom was when he was the fourth-best pitcher on his high school team. That photo was my way of saying to Tom, "See, Tom? I was good once! Like you!" I have always wondered over the forty years of our friendship why it wasn't enough for me that I knew how good a pitcher I had once been. Why did I still need Tom's validation?

When I called Tom to ask if he had gotten that photo, he said, "I got it. You were a cocky sonuvabitch even then."

"Yes, I was, Tom. I thought the Braves would keep me in Milwaukee at eighteen. When they sent me to McCook, Nebraska, in the Class D rookie league I was furious."

"I can imagine."

Nancy and Anne come into Tom's office. Nancy gives me a hug and a kiss on the cheek. I say, "You don't have to say it, Nancy. I know. I haven't changed a bit."

She looks at my white hair and white beard, flutters her eyelashes, and says, "Pat, you haven't changed a bit." We all laugh.

I say, "I heard you've become quite the businesswoman."

"Well," she says, "for years I was just eye candy."

I say, "Nancy, you were never *just* eye candy." She had been a tanned, beautiful California blonde when I first met her in 1971. She still was beautiful, in her sixties, with her blonde hair and her sharp cheekbones that could be Slavic or Native American. In all the times I met her, I always came away with one impression of her. A sly remove. She was enigmatic, unreadable, like January Jones in *Mad Men*. Her husband was the obvious one, a big, emotional, blustering teenager. Nancy was the mystery.

We talk some, explaining to Anne how we'd known each other for forty years but haven't seen each other much in the past twenty. A lot of my communication with Tom was over the phone when he was still pitching. I tell Anne, "I use to call up your father after a game and tell him what he'd done wrong on the mound."

Anne gives me her mother's sly smile and says, "That must have gone over big with Dad."

"Your father's always been jealous of me because I threw harder than him."

Nancy tilts her head slightly and says, "Really? I didn't know that, Pat."

"Absolutely, Nancy. Of course, he'll never admit it."

Tom bellows, "Yeah, and between you and me we won three hundred and eleven games."

"I tell everyone that."

Anne looks at her mother and says, "Dumb and Dumber." We all agree that Tom is the laid-back Jeff Daniels character and I am the hyper, obnoxious Jim Carrey character.

As Anne and Nancy leave, Nancy says, "Thomas, don't forget your sunblock when you go outside."

Tom and I go out to the back deck that looks out over his property on a brilliantly sunny afternoon that is now hot. His terraced vineyards are off to our left, his swimming pool below us, and the Napa Valley and the Palisades Mountains around it off in the distance. He says he'd found these 116 acres that were undiscovered because they were all overgrown, trees, scrub. He cleared the land, got in water and electricity, had his house built by a Harvard architect named Ken Kao, and laid out his vines.

"The grapes get the south sun," he says, "which is a big deal, apparently."

Today, his Seaver Vineyards is a small, highly respected boutique winery that produces about six hundred cases a year. He makes a good profit, enough to live on. "I wasn't afraid to do this," he says. "I didn't want to go to the end of my life not doing it and wishing I had done it. I don't want to retire, but now the winery is pretty self-sufficient. I'll probably turn it over to the family in a few years, but there's not much more we can do with it. The next thing I want to do is paint. I want to paint these mountains, but I could never paint at the level of Diebenkorn. You know, I used to draw pictures when I was on the road in my playing days." Pitching, the vineyards, painting pictures—they all have in common that they are endeavors of a reclusive man.

As a kid of nine I used to collect stamps. I would take three buses into Bridgeport and stop at each of the city's three stamp shops. I'd buy new issues from foreign countries I'd never heard of, old canceled United States stamps that reeked of age, and some old foreign stamps, too, mostly from Italy, my heritage. I spent hours in my bedroom putting those stamps into albums. I used to draw, too. Like Tom, I wanted to become an artist. My parents bought me a draftsman's drawing board for my bedroom. I'd spend hours there with my stamps, and now drawing pictures, too, of my collie, Lady, and copying pictures out of magazines. One night when I was ten, I stayed up late and copied a drawing of a woman in a magazine by an artist named Vargas. My copy was so perfect I couldn't wait to show my parents. But the next morning it was gone. I knew my parents must have taken it. But why? I had a vague idea why, but at ten I could not define that reason. Neither my parents nor I ever mentioned that drawing.

Putting stamps in an album and drawing pictures in an empty room, pitching on that isolated mound, then writing for fifty years in still another empty room. Seventy years of a reclusive life. No wonder Tom and I get along. We have that same reclusive nature to be alone that finds its only outlet in an infrequent and distant friendship of like-minded men who never want to get too close.

I don't tell Tom the story about my drawing. I learned my lesson after my Roland Hemond story.

I ask Tom if it was hard to convince Nancy to leave Greenwich and New York City to come out here to this seclusion. He says, "She was a little uncertain. We had this beautiful renovated barn in Greenwich, antique furniture, her garden club, bowling team. But I told her I had to see if I could do this. If I stayed in Greenwich, I'd be Tom Seaver for the rest of my life. I'd die there. Now, she's bought into it. She has her house here and she's part of something with the business." He glances at me. "I'm not supposed to wear shoes in the house. I can't bring my dogs in either. I used to sleep with my dogs when I was a kid in Fresno because we had no heat. Imagine, me, a kid from Fresno, in New York City. You know they're going to name a street after me in Fresno. 'Seaver Way.'" He goes silent for a moment, looking out over his property. Finally, he says, "This was a blank palette when I first saw it. Now it's the most exciting thing I've ever done."

Before we go to the vineyards, where Tom has to "do some work," he wants to show me something. He points down to the lip of the swimming pool, the edge of the pool overgrown with brush that is falling down the mountain. "A sculpture I bought in Cincinnati one year," he says.

We walk down the steep steps to the pool. I had slipped on my stairs the day before I'd come to California and hurt my leg. Tom's limping, too. We both hobble down the stairs and walk to the end of the pool. I step up on the lip to walk around to the sculpture. The lip is very narrow. Tom says, "If you fall in the pool, I'm not jumping in to save you." So instead, we both walk through the brush that slopes down, holding on to each other's arm so we won't fall.

CHAPTER TEN

2013

PART III

Ten minutes later, after we left his swimming pool, Tom and I are walking between the rows of vines, up and down the steep terraces in the hot sun. Tom's three Labrador retrievers romp around us. Big, playful, doofus dogs with their tongues hanging out. He tells me their names. Major, Bandy, Brix.

I say, "Bricks, like in chimney bricks?"

"No, Brix."

"Bricks?"

"No, Brix."

"Who's on first?" He doesn't get it, so I say, "Spell it."

"B-R-I-X. It's French for the sugar content in grapes." We stop at a vine drooping with clusters of grapes. He snips off a cluster and hands it to me. I hold the grapes over my head like a Roman emperor at an orgy and eat the small, black, sweet grapes off the cluster. "Delicious," I say, wiping purple juice from my mouth with the back of my hand.

Tom goes into a long explanation about the varieties of grapes on his vines. How each vine's grapes had different characteristics that you could only tell by tasting them. That's why each row was numbered.

"Very good, Thomas. You always did explain things precise."

"Ly," he says. "Precise-*ly*. You're supposed to be the fucking writer, and you don't know your grammar."

"OK. Precise-*ly*."

"Thank you very much. You know, I got a journalism degree from USC." Irony of ironies! Tom Seaver trying to impress me.

"Yeah, and I had a better fastball than you."

But he ignores me. "I was always like that about pitching. I had to be precise. I couldn't just mail it *in*!" Then he begins to explain more about his vines, about the cordon and proper height for each vine. I tune him out and eat my grapes, the juice running down my sweatshirt. He looks at me, annoyed, and says, "Pay attention. I'm gonna give you a fucking lesson."

"I don't want a fucking lesson."

"That doesn't matter. I'm giving you one. Now, if the secondary fruit grows too high, you have to snip it off or else they'll take energy from the vines."

I feign interest. "How high?"

"Each row has to be only to a height of fourteen."

"Fourteen what? Inches? Feet?"

"I don't know. It's just a standard height. Stop asking questions and just listen. This is important, damn it. If you didn't talk so much, you might learn something. If the vines are too high, you have to trim them." He reaches up with his snips and trims a vine.

"Oh, I see. The height of each vine is a template for the row. Your job is to go down the row, trimming the tops to make them conform to the template. I can see how the monotony of this appeals to your BORING, PRECISE, FUCKING METHODICAL NATURE."

"Bullshit. You think too much. You always did."

"I had a better fastball than you."

"In your dreams."

"I did."

"Yeah, and between us we won three hundred and eleven major league games."

"Absa-fucking-lutely! I tell everybody that!"

It has not escaped me all these years that Tom's and my vaudeville routine—Frick and Frack, Butch and Sundance, Abbott and Costello, "Who's on first?"—might seem tiresome to others. Childish even. But it's always been our way of connecting with each other after long absences. We don't know how each other's lives have unfolded during those absences. Happiness, tragedy, Sarah's Hodgkin's disease, my wife's breast cancer. When I'm interviewing Tom for a story, we don't talk about those things, except in a general way. I ask him if he's happy. He'll say, "Yes. I have my wife, my kids, my grandkids, my dogs, my work in the vineyards. And you?" I say, "The same. Wife, and dogs, and my work." He'll say, "That's all anyone needs." Then we'll slip quickly into our vaudeville routine as if embarrassed by our small intimacies. Tom assumes the role of the long-suffering and stoic Sundance Kid burdened by the incessant questions, interruptions, and delusions of past glory of Butch Cassidy. Tom: "You just keep thinking, Pat. That's what you're good at." Me: "I got vision, Tom, and the rest of the world wears bifocals."

I ask him if he'd still have his vineyards if he hadn't missed out on today's big baseball paydays. Tom only made a million dollars a year the last three years of his career. (It occurs to me as I write this about poor Tom, only three years of $1 million paydays, how easily I slip into a famous baseball player's mindset about money. A million dollars only three times in twenty years! My best years as a writer earned me maybe $100,000 a year, so much money to me then that I used to tell my father, "Yeah, Dad, I'm lighting my cigars with C-notes these days.")

Yet if Tom Seaver were pitching today, he'd be making over $30 million a year. Did he resent missing out on those big paydays?

"It use to bother me," he says. "But I got over it."

He says he quit pitching at forty-two because "I started to lose interest. I wanted to go home. I couldn't do it anymore. I never was pissed I missed the big paydays. Be careful what you wish for—you might get it. If I'd made that thirty million dollars a year, maybe I'd just have bought that huge, finished vineyard and let others do it all. I'd have missed out on the pleasure of being in the vineyards every day. My pleasure has always been in the work, not the ego."

Which is true only in the reflections of an old man. As a young man, Tom told me he pitched so that he would one day be recognized as the greatest pitcher who ever lived. As for his lost big paydays, they were the result of his ego, too. He always insisted that he negotiate his contracts with teams without an agent because, a friend of his told me, "He liked to look his GMs in the eyes to get a read on them." A facile answer I'm not sure I believe. Tom was always about the money. He just wasn't very good at intuiting where baseball salaries were headed a few years after he signed his latest contract.

After Tom retired, his agent Matt Merola would often get big-money offers from book publishers for Tom to write the definitive Tom Seaver autobiography. Merola turned them down because Tom didn't want to write such a personal, in-depth book about himself. Besides, Merola said that Tom could make a lot more money (i.e., without the effort of all that introspection an autobiography demands) by just signing autographs for fans.

That was a sad image for me to conjure. Tom hated to sit at a desk. He was contemptuous of fans' intrusion into his life. A longtime friend of Tom's told me once that Tom built a wall around himself to keep out the media and the fans. When they approached him, "He'd give them a dirty look. Then later, with intimates, he would laugh over how he intimidated those people." And here he was now, in retirement, sitting for hours at a card table in a crowded shopping mall, like a caged geek at a carnival, smiling, chitchatting and glad-handing an endless line of strangers, while he scrawled his signature across photos of his former self, the only self that really mattered to him, in a baseball uniform. And for what? Easy money, which it never is. Easy.

I tell Tom that when I first got to Calistoga, I asked people in town where Tom Seaver's vineyards were. Nobody knew. I said, "You do know Tom Seaver lives here?" They shrugged. I said, "You do know who Tom Seaver is, don't you?" No.

"I like it like that," he says, "not being known. I put up an emotional barrier. You know, Stan Musial used to say hello to everybody. I can't do that. It's all one way with me. I'd rather learn about someone else than be Tom Seaver. Oh, you're an ankle doctor. Where'd you go to school? Was your dad a doctor? No? He was a coal miner?" He looks at me and says, "Now you got a pretty good story. I love the story stuff."

I don't tell him what I'm thinking. Yeah, Tom, strangers maybe. But not me. You never ask me about my life: "Tell me, Pat, what made you decide to become a writer?" Then I realize I'm being small-minded. Tom has always been interested in what I think. He just knows that, sooner or later, I'll tell him what I think without him having to ask. He knows me that well, the sonuvabitch!

"A pretty good story?" I say. "You mean rising action, climax, and denouement." He looks at me as if I am speaking a foreign language. I say, "I got that from Susie. She was a theater actress for years. I used to read her scripts."

"Baseball is theater, too. Only no script. McCovey has a say in the action, not only me. I use to keep a notebook for each game, the pitches I'd thrown."

I tell him that Susie approached her plays with the same methodical mindset as he approached his games. "She used to memorize all the other actors' lines in case they forgot them. In this one play, she was a wife suspected of murdering her husband. The actor playing the detective forgot his lines, so she fed them to him. 'So, Inspector, I guess you're here to question me about my husband's murder?' The actor nodded. She said, 'I suppose you want to know where I was last night?' The actor nodded. It went on like that the whole play."

Tom says, "I knew I'd like her." Then he says he deliberately kept his "world small" so that his entire focus would be on baseball. In a way, Tom was even a recluse at the height of his fame. He did not want much to do with the world beyond baseball. He cultivated a studied dullness beyond baseball. But inside the game, Tom was a gregarious guy with his teammates.

When Tom was with the White Sox, he had a lot in common with their catcher, Pudge Fisk. Both men have been married all their adult lives to the same woman they married in their early twenties. Tom cultivated grapes, which he called "my babies." Fisk cultivated orchids in a greenhouse, cross-breeding them until they "pollinated, got stretch marks, then nine months later they flower." Tom and Pudge were almost indistinguishable in appearance, too. Big, muscular, handsome, pale-skinned guys with sandy-colored hair, always clean shaven. Both were hardworking blue-collar kind of guys with an angry edge that Tom tried to hide. Fisk didn't.

During his twenty-three years as a big league catcher, possibly the greatest catcher ever in baseball, first with the Red Sox, then the White Sox, Fisk seemed always angry, at everyone. At fans wanting him to autograph their Carlton Fisk T-shirt. ("You just happened to have it with you, huh?") At people who ask him personal questions. ("Why the fuck should I tell you?") At paperboys who toss his morning paper on his snow-covered driveway instead of his front porch. ("The next morning, I waited for him. I told him, 'Do it right, or don't deliver it again.'") At drivers who litter, which is why his SUV looks as if he slept and ate in it for months. ("I *never* throw anything out the window.") At ballplayers whose girlfriends pose half naked for photographs. ("Her tits all pushed together!") At maudlin country and western music. ("All that 'my wife left me and my dog died' shit, it drags me down.") At being defined in his later years as an old catcher. ("I hate that, being defined by age, not talent. My wife's dog is fifteen. Sure, he doesn't have the fire anymore. Like a lot of us. But, hey, we're still valuable.")

He's angry at sportswriters who don't use tape recorders ("They make you slow down, lose your train of thought"), and other reporters who created a rivalry between himself and the Yankee catcher, Thurman Munson. ("Because I was tall and handsome and he was squat and ugly and always in the dirt. I was in the dirt, *too!* I just looked cleaner.") He's angry at computers that tell you "facts" about a hitter but not what the catcher "feels" about the batter at a given moment in a game. He's angry at players who are immature and coddled, while he's never been "stroked," never gotten "respect," and players who are "selfish," like Deion Sanders of the Braves and Yankees. ("ME! ME! ME! I! I! I! His selfishness *offends* me!")

When Sanders was with the Yankees one year, he stepped into the batter's box with Fisk catching. Sanders, who referred to himself as "Prime Time" and "Neon Deion," drew a dollar sign in the dirt with his bat. Then he hit a routine infield pop fly. Sanders stood at the plate, watching the ball drop into a fielder's glove. Fisk snapped at him, "Run the fucking ball out, you piece of shit!" Fisk laughs, remembering that moment. "He was offended," Fisk says. "I don't know why." The next time he came to bat, Sanders said to Fisk, "The days of slavery are over." Fisk ripped off his mask and lunged at Sanders' throat with his hands. He would have been the first player to strangle an opposing batter to death, right there, in front of thirty thousand fans, if the home plate umpire had not stopped him. "He was trying to make a race thing out of it," Fisk says. "I was just trying to tell him there was a right way and a wrong way to play this game."

Fisk has even been angry at himself at times, when he felt he had mishandled one of his pitchers. When Hall of Fame pitcher Ferguson Jenkins was with the Red Sox, Fisk says, "I did him a disservice. I never felt I called the game right for him. I…aw…I don't know. We coulda had a lot of fun."

Fisk was always most angry at the baseball executives with the Red Sox and White Sox, who, he felt, mismanaged his career. He once threw his helmet at his Red Sox manager who questioned his pitch calling. He also kicked down the door of a Red Sox GM who questioned his team loyalty. Fisk grew up in New Hampshire, a flinty New Englander whose dream it was always to play his entire career with the Red Sox. Which didn't mean he'd let those Red Sox executives disrespect him. In 1980, he raged at Red Sox GM Haywood Sullivan for not paying his players (i.e., Fisk) what they were worth. Sullivan retaliated by sending out Fisk's 1981 contract one day after the deadline for sending out contracts had passed. Which made Fisk a free agent. So he signed a $3.5 million contract with the White Sox and almost immediately began tormenting their executives, like Jerry Reinsdorf, who called Fisk "a prima donna" and "a baby [who] doesn't like anybody and is always unhappy." Fisk replied that Reinsdorf must have been looking in the mirror. Then he admitted, "I guess I do have a reputation as a grouch." Which is why the White Sox media staff always warned reporters that Fisk could be "difficult, moody," when they really meant "unhinged."

By the time Seaver arrived in Chicago in '85, Fisk had mellowed a bit, at least as far as his interactions with fans went. He had actually become a favorite in Chicago, whose blue-collar fans appreciated the hard-nosed way Fisk played the game. He also had a new like-minded teammate in Seaver, and the two men gravitated to one another. They went out to dinner together on the road and sometimes in Chicago. Fisk was easily recognizable in Chicago, where he'd played for four years before Tom arrived in '85. One night, Tom and Fisk were eating dinner at an exclusive Chicago restaurant. A male fan approached their table hesitantly. He glanced at the two men, from one to the other, than back again. Finally, he shoved a piece of paper and pen toward Tom and said, "Could you please give me your autograph Mr. Fisk?" Tom backhanded the paper and pen and screamed at the man, "No fuckin' way! Can't you see we're eating dinner? Get the fuck outta here!" Years later, when Fisk told me that story, he said, "That was great for my image, wasn't it? But Tom didn't care. He thought he was hysterical." He smiled, then added, "I caught Tom's three hundredth win, you know. Tom taught me a lot. An awareness that there are things other than physical talent that were important in the game. He knew his limitations. When it was time to quit. I only know my limitations when I run into them." He shook his head and added, "Aw, I'm not the brightest guy in the world."

Unlike Seaver, however, Fisk always said he never had time for friendships in the clubhouse. It was just a place to prepare for work. Tom liked the clubhouse, his refuge from his solitary life away from it. He liked playing it fast and loose in the company of men with a common interest, baseball. It was his man cave, as long as he didn't have to get too close to his fellow cave dwellers.

Marty Appel, a longtime Yankees media executive, co-wrote two books with Tom in the '80s, *Great Moments in Baseball* and *Tom Seaver's All-Time Baseball Greats*. Marty told me, "I was a big fan of Tom's. I really admired him. When I interviewed him for those books, it was as good as it gets. Me and Tom talking outside on his lawn on a sunny afternoon at his farmhouse in Greenwich. Nancy bringing us lemonade. I thought we were equals. Friends. But I realized that, to Tom, I was just one of his employees. He never returned my calls. Nancy did. Tom had no respect for me. I asked him once to give me the names of some of his close friends. He couldn't give me one name."

George Grande, a baseball TV broadcaster for over twenty years, was a freshman on USC's baseball team when Tom was the team's star.

He told me, "I got a hit off Tom once in an intra-squad game. After the game Tom told me, 'I coulda punched you out [struck him out] if I wanted to.' That's the way he was. I consider Tom my close friend, going on fifty years now. Once in a while we'd meet in New York City. But in all those years, my wife and I never socialized at his Greenwich house with Tom and Nancy. They put up a wall to keep you at arm's length. Tom had no time for you if he didn't buy in to your act."

CHAPTER ELEVEN

2013

PART IV

For Tom Seaver, a baseball clubhouse was a respite from his nature. Now, on this hot, dry day at his mountaintop vineyard in Calistoga, left to his own devices, Tom's letting his reclusive nature take over his life. Long, solitary days in the vineyards. They may be good for his psyche, but not for his Lyme disease. He can't exercise his memory if each day in solitude is like the last. But this day, Tom is not in solitude. So he talks.

As we walk among the vines, Tom tells me a story apropos of nothing. He was twenty-eight, at the height of his fame with the Mets. One day he was pitching a game so superbly that its result was a foregone conclusion, to him, at least. He went into the clubhouse between innings to change his shirt, and the "clubhouse kid" told him, "Players aren't supposta be here between innings." Tom tells me, "That kid always use ta bust my chops, so I asked if he wanted to play a game of gin rummy." They played gin while Tom kept his ear tuned to the game on the radio. When it was his time to go back out to the mound, he warned the kid, "Don't you dare look at my cards, I'll be right back."

He got three quick outs and returned to his clubhouse card game. He tells me, "It was one of those days, Pat. Give me a run and the game's done. I got back to the clubhouse and asked the kid if he'd looked at my cards. He said no, so we began again. Then my roomie, Buddy Harrelson, came in. He saw me and said, 'Roomie, what're you doin'?' I told him I was playing rummy between innings. What's it look like? Buddy shook his head and said, 'Man, you're crazy!' I said, 'Now, that's a different issue.'"

The point of that seemingly pointless story, to me anyway, is how Tom remembers those trivial moments in baseball with such clarity and affection. Which makes me wonder why someone like Tom, who loved the game so much, not only the pitching, but every nuance of it, had turned his back on it.

We pause at a vine. Tom tells me something about the grapes on this particular vine. He looks at me. He says, "You don't give a shit, do you?"

"Is it that obvious?" He shakes his head in disgust. I say, "What I would like to know, Big Guy, is why you never stayed in the game after you retired."

He says, "For the same reason you didn't become a pitching coach. Because no one ever asked me." And he was too proud to ask them. I don't blame him. He was, after all, Tom Fucking Seaver, the greatest pitcher of his age.

♠ ♠ ♠

Howie Rose, a Mets TV broadcaster in the late '90s, told me, "I always wondered why the Mets never asked Tom to do anything for them after he retired. Why not recruit Tom as a manager, GM, or Mets president? Maybe even the commissioner of baseball."

George Grande told me the answer to Rose's question was a simple one. "Mets executives were afraid of Tom," George said. "He was always the smartest guy in the room, so they would not let him in.

Tom had offers to be a pitching coach or a manager, but not from the Mets. The '90s were a sad time for Tom. He wanted to be a part of the Mets. He wanted to be the architect of the Mets. It bothered him the Mets didn't let him into the Mets family. They just wanted Tom to show up every once in a while, wave to fans, sign some autographs, and then leave. I thought that was the biggest mistake the Mets ever made, not realizing how important Tom could be for them."

While Tom was waiting for a Mets offer that never came, he kept his hand in the game by broadcasting baseball games on TV in New York throughout the '90s. His first TV gig was with the Yankees.

"I hired Tom to broadcast Yankee games in eighty-nine," Marty Appel told me. "It wasn't for a lot of money, low hundred thousands. I felt the Mets didn't want him broadcasting their games because he left too big a footprint. We had a big press conference to announce Tom as the new Yankees broadcaster. He gave a little speech in which he referred to himself in the third person. The Yankee fans never embraced him because he'd been a Met. That's when the experience turned dark."

Another Yankees front office executive described Tom's TV baseball broadcasting as "pedestrian. Tom just phoned it in. He wasn't inclined to go down on the field and do player interviews. He never cultivated a relationship with the Yankee rank and file. He didn't even say hello to the little people, like the secretaries. He just walked right by them. Tom could have brought a lot more to his Yankee TV experience, but he didn't."

Finally, in 1999, the Mets felt that enough time and distance had passed from that great unpleasantness of the Midnight Massacre and their blunder of leaving Tom off their protected list in 1983, when the White Sox signed him. So they brought him back to Shea Stadium as a Mets TV broadcaster to work with Ralph Kiner and Howie Rose. "I was so thrilled to work with Tom in '99," said Rose. "He was a hero to me when I was thirteen. I remember a game we worked in St. Louis.

Tom called a balk on air before the umpire did. It was a shame he never revealed himself on the air, though."

Tim McCarver, a twenty-year baseball TV broadcaster after his twenty-year catching career, told me, "I never worked with Tom on TV. He was always Tom Seaver, the pitcher, to me." I asked McCarver if he'd heard any of the games Tom worked as a broadcaster. He said, "Yes…I would not praise him as a broadcaster."

● ● ●

Tom's tired now, after walking up and down the rows of vines in his vineyard in the hot sun. He says, "Let's go sit in my office." His vineyard office is a circle of trees with two chairs in the open space in the center of the trees. We sit there in the cool shade. His Labs lie around us and go to sleep.

"They've got to be the laziest dogs," I say.

"That's the way to get on my bad side. Dissing my dogs."

"But they don't do anything."

"They do when they have to. Chase away the deer and scare off the coyotes. All I have to say to them is one word. 'Kill!'" We sit there for a few minutes, and then he says, "I come here when it's hot and I'm tired. I do the crossword puzzles." He looks at me. "I don't believe the way I'm talking today relative to three months ago."

I have not asked Tom anything about his Lyme disease. I don't want to know. How it affects him. Debilitates him. Things he can no longer do, remember, enjoy. His prognosis for the future. I am selfish. I want him to be the Tom Seaver I always knew, will always remember. So when he brings up his disease, I play him off, change the subject.

I ask him what was the turning point in his life when he was a kid.

He says, "When I joined the Marines, I was seventeen." Tom had been just an average-sized kid in high school, and only the third- or fourth-best pitcher on his team. "All I cared about was baseball," he said. "I was not a good student. Fractions to me were like the Rosetta Stone.

I failed advanced algebra in my junior year. My dad was not happy. So I went to summer school, worked my butt off, and got a D. My teacher said, 'I'll give you a C if you promise never to take another math course in your life.'"

So, after high school, with no professional baseball or college offers, he joined the Marines. He got taller, heavier, stronger, and most of all, he says, "I learned discipline, discipline, discipline. Somebody says, 'Do it,' you do it, and eventually you come out the other end and you're proud." He also came out the other end with an improved fastball, too. Then, after a summer pitching in the Alaskan collegiate league, he returned to California with an explosive fastball that got him a scholarship to USC and later, a bonus contract with the Mets. He won 16 games in his first year with the Mets, a lousy team, and was voted Rookie of the Year. He never looked back.

I ask him who were his idols in those days. I expect him to mention some pitchers, like Sandy Koufax or Robin Roberts. He says, "My older brother, Charles. He was a beautiful man. Six-four, dark hair like my dad. He had a huge intellect. He wrote poetry. He was a sculptor. He lived in Lower Manhattan. Whenever he'd see me pitch, he always asked me the same question: 'What does it feel like to strike out fourteen batters?' I told him it all had to do with how I prepared for a game, how my brain went to a different level three days before I faced a batter, how I created a situation in a game I prepared for. I explained it in artistic terms for him, like it was an artwork you created physically and mentally." He looks across at me and says, "Charles died of cancer when he was fifty-five." There are tears in his eyes. "I miss him so much."

We get up and walk back to my car in silence. I understood now why Tom was so dismissive of abstract intellectualism. It was Charles's province. Tom would not intrude on it. His brother was the brain. So Tom mapped out for himself a physical persona. The methodical hard worker. Before I leave, Tom tells me to come back the next morning at

6:30 to watch the sun come up over the mountain with him. It was his ritual every day before he went to work in the vineyards in the cool, gray morning. Then, as I back my car out, I see him take out a worn little notebook from his jeans pocket. He writes down my name, the date, and the time I'd arrive the next morning.

⬟ ⬟ ⬟

The next morning, in darkness, Tom and I are standing in his vineyards staring off at the mountains, waiting for the sun. His three Labs snuffle around us. Tom's drinking his coffee, I'm smoking my cigar. He looks at it and says, "You're gonna burn down the whole fucking mountain." So I let it go out. We stand side by side like two old savages waiting for the miracle of the sun they don't understand. To pass the time, Tom asks me if he'd ever told me his Ron Hunt story. I say no, but Hunt had been my teammate one year in the Braves' minor leagues in 1959. He went on to a nice thirteen-year career in the majors, mostly with the Mets. He was famous for crowding the plate to get hit by pitches.

Tom says, "I faced him this one time and threw him a high inside fastball. I followed through and lost sight of him. When I looked up, there was a pop fly over my head. I caught it for an out. And then I looked back to home plate, and there was Ron sprawled in the dirt, unconscious."

"Hunt was a pain in the ass to pitch to," I say, "always crowding the plate, slapping foul balls. He drove me nuts. You did good hitting the sonuvabitch in the head. I tried to hit him once in a spring training game. Didn't even come close. Walked him on four pitches." Tom laughs. I look at him. "You think it's funny, Seaver? It wouldn't be so funny if it had been your fucking career."

Just then the sun comes up on cue, click, like stage lights in a theater. It's a pale, reddish-blue color on an overcast day. Tom's disappointed. He'd wanted me to see it in all its fiery glory. Still, the sun's pale light on the vineyards is eerie and beautiful, the vines all darkish shadows without color, until the sun rises higher and they become a dark green flecked with purple, like a French impressionist painting.

Tom says, "In a way, I'm painting this vineyard as if it was my artwork."

"Yeah, well, I'm doing the same with you, Big Guy. You're like this big, blank block of marble I'm chipping away at. I'm gonna sculpt my masterpiece. A Seaver."

"So you're Michelangelo now?"

"Yeah. But I'll call my masterpiece *The Thomas*." I am very serious in my way. When I saw *David* in Florence one year with Susie, I told her it reminded me of Tom. I explained to her that critics have been arguing for hundreds of years over whether David had just thrown his rock at Goliath or was about to throw it. The moment I saw *David*, I knew he was about to throw from a pitcher's stretch motion with runners on base. He was standing sideways to Goliath, his left leg slightly forward, most of his weight shifted on his right leg, his right shoulder tilted down, his right arm hanging loose by his side, his head turned, getting ready to throw his fastball, glancing over his left shoulder toward Goliath, smiling, who, in his mammoth dimness, sees only a pretty boy with curls. Goliath doesn't notice that look in David's eyes, or if he does, he misconstrues it as a look of fear. But it's not fear. It's that scary look certain pitchers have in their eyes before they throw their 98-mph fastball inches from the batter's head. Jiggle his eyeballs a little. Send the batter a message. Make him contemplate mortality. You're smiling at me, cocksucker! This one's gonna be in your fucking ear! And it was.

That statue reminded me of Tom.

Tom looks embarrassed, as he often does when I talk seriously about him. He prefers I be a smart-ass with him, like guys in the locker room.

For the next hour I let Tom work in silence. I watch him go up and down the rows, picking up bits of paper or plastic, anything that mars the beauty of his artwork. He studies the top of a vine that's maybe an inch higher than the rest of the row. Then he snips it to fit the template. He reminds me of the farmer in Robert Frost's poem, who says, "Good fences make good neighbors." But who was Tom keeping out? He was such a contradiction. A recluse who loved the company of men. Was he lonely up here? I remembered how he reacted when I told him about Justin Verlander yesterday at breakfast. He asked me a dozen questions about Verlander. I told him how Verlander and I had argued over who was better, today's players or players from my generation and before. He said today's players were better hitters, with their short, compact swings, compared to the longer swings of Ted Williams and Joe DiMaggio. Tom piped up, "Yeah, but those older guys had multiple swings, depending on the situation. Today's hitters have just one swing, for the fences." I told him Verlander was a tough pitcher. Great overhand fastball and curve. But he wasn't as smart as Tom, or as disciplined. When he got in trouble, he didn't know what to do except just throw harder. Tom said, "He sounds like my kinda guy. An old-time pitcher." Then he looked at me and said, "Do you know him well?" I said, "Well enough. Why?" Tom said, as if a little embarrassed, "Maybe the next time you talk to him you could tell him I'd like to talk to him. He could come up and visit sometime."

"Sure," I say. A few months later, during spring training, I went up to Verlander at his locker in the Tigers clubhouse. I told him about Tom, how Tom was a fan of his pitching. "Tom said he'd love to talk to you about pitching if you ever come to the San Francisco area," I said. Verlander looked at me. I handed him a piece of paper with Tom's telephone number on it. "Call him," I said. "He's a great guy." Verlander laughed, a breath, and tossed the paper into his locker.

When it's fully light, we walk back to Tom's truck to go into town. We're going to meet the photographer, Kelley, who would take Tom's picture this morning. She'd driven up from Berkeley, so we told her we'd buy her breakfast at the deli.

I get into the passenger side of his truck. "Jeez, this thing is filthy," I say. "I'm gonna have to burn my clothes tonight."

"I like it this way."

"Yeah, so everyone will know you're a workingman." He drives the truck onto Diamond Mountain Road and we move down the steep, curvy, dangerous road. I say, "You know, I worked construction once. When I came back from baseball, I dug ditches. I learned there's an art to digging an even ditch. You don't stab the shovel at the dirt with your arms. You use your leg, pushing the shovel into the dirt with your foot."

He looks across at me. "And I never figured that out? There was a reason they put a little flange on the shovel? All these years I was doing it wrong until you just told me how to do it right."

"I'm glad I taught you something."

"Yeah, the Art of Shovelry."

"Whoo! Big Guy, watch where the fuck you're going! You're gonna drive us off this fucking mountain."

Still looking at me with an evil grin, he says, "*Now* you're gonna teach me how to drive, too?"

"Yeah, and then I'll teach you how to pitch."

"Good. I'll teach you how to write. You don't even know proper grammar."

"Fuck you."

The trees hanging over the road like a canopy make it seem as if we're still driving in darkness. We must have been thinking the same thing.

Tom says, "The woods are lovely, dark and deep."

"And we have miles to go before we sleep...so keep your eyes on the road."

"I thought I'd give you a little something to make you feel good about yourself."

We eat breakfast with Kelley, the photographer. She's in her twenties, tall, slim, blonde, a dead ringer for the actress Shelley Duvall, except Kelley is more beautiful. She picks at her food while Tom and I perform for her, two bratty schoolkids sniping at each other, Frick and Frack, Tom and Huck, the Katzenjammer Kids, Dumb and Dumber, the list is endless. While we rag each other, Kelley surreptitiously raises her camera and snaps our picture. She seems not to know what to make of these two old guys acting like lovesick schoolboys trying to charm her. What were we going to do next, pull her hair? She had assumed, at least, that this writer and this famous baseball pitcher would be grown-ups!

After breakfast, Kelley follows Tom's truck up Diamond Mountain Road in her Prius. Tom drives more slowly now so she can keep up. We talk. I bring up the Midnight Massacre. Tom had been pitching superbly for the Mets for ten years when Mets chairman M. Donald Grant conspired with *New York Daily News* columnist Dick Young to run Tom out of New York. Their pretext was that Tom had gotten uppity and was no longer content with his place on the team. Tom was asking for more money. Grant complained that Tom was an ingrate. He belittled his union activities by calling Tom and Marvin Miller, the union lawyer, "communists." The contradiction seemed to elude the clueless Grant. Seaver was both a "communist" for his union activities and a greedy capitalist for asking for more money. Grant even implied that Seaver, who had recently been admitted to the Greenwich Country Club, was a presumptuous parvenu who was trying to rise above his station in life, presumably that station being a "dumb jock." But mostly Grant was furious that Tom was known in New York as "the Franchise." Grant screamed at Seaver once, "*I'm* 'the

Franchise!'" Finally, Tom had had enough of Grant and Young and, in an emotional outburst, demanded a trade to the Cincinnati Reds.

I remind Tom of *my* Dick Young story, when I spoke to the University of Delaware sports journalism class a few weeks after Young did in the late '70s.

"Dick Young was the most disgusting human being I ever met," says Tom. This is the first time in all the years I have known Tom that I have ever heard him speak with such fury about another human being.

When we reach the mountaintop, Tom checks in his rearview mirror to make sure Kelley is behind us, then he turns down his driveway. He's quiet for a moment, as if something has been bothering him all these years. Finally, he says, serious now, "Did you really throw harder than me?"

I laugh. "Thomas! It's finally dawning on you." He looks embarrassed. I can see in his eyes that this is important to Tom. I say, "All kidding aside. The truth? Maybe, maybe not. There were no radar guns in my day. We had to guess. My best shot was ninety-six, ninety-seven, maybe ninety-eight. No faster than you, Thomas. But I had a great overhand curve. Straight down. If I didn't throw it in the dirt or over the batter's head, it was unhittable." Tom laughs now. I said, "My manager called it 'the Unfair One.' What was unfair was to have such a pitch and be so clueless how to make it work for me."

I am lying, of course. I did have a bit more control over my curveball than I admit to Tom. I wasn't that wild! I did have an idea. I am lying, too, about my fastball. I did have a better fastball than Tom's when I was nineteen, in the Midwest League. I was lying, too, when Tom couldn't remember I had pancakes for breakfast, and I told him it was just age, I forget, too, we're old guys now. I'm a writer. It's my job not to forget details, no matter how insignificant they might seem. You never can tell when you might use those details. But the truth is inconsequential to me now, compared to my need to protect

Tom from his fading memory, and my superior fastball. So, for the first time in my life, and certainly the first time with Tom, I diminish myself for him.

While Tom poses for Kelley in the rows of his grapevines, I go into his "vineyard office" in the midst of the trees. I sit there and watch Tom pose, smile, it all coming back to him now, the right camera angle, one hand on his hip, the other draped over a vine, slouchy-hipped, so natural in a way only famous people can be who are used to cameras being aimed at them…while Kelley, backpedaling, snaps his picture. Tom's Labs surround me. They put their paws on my lap and lick my face. One of them gets up behind me, puts his big paws on my shoulders, and tries to pull me backward off the chair. I snap at them all, "SIT! Goddamn it!" They all sit! Amazing! My Shiba Inus ignore my commands as if deaf. Except when I open the biscuit jar, which they hear from the far reaches of the lawn and come running into the house. THEN they sit! Tom's Labs stare up at me with pitiful eyes, their tails wagging obsequiously as if seeking forgiveness. I feel guilty, so I pick up a stick and throw it into the woods. They charge after it, squabbling over it, until one of them swipes it from the others and brings it back to me to throw again. When I reach for it, he pulls it back from me. Then I hear Tom's voice call out. "Done!"

We all walk back to the cars, the dogs jumping on me, trying to get me to throw the stick again. But I'll have none of it.

We stand around the cars for a few minutes while Kelley snaps a few more pictures of me and Tom. To pass the time, Tom says, "Did I ever tell you my Boomer story?"

Boomer had been a young catcher with the White Sox when Tom was approaching his three hundredth victory. One night, Boomer started the game whacked out on greenies. He was so zonked that he forgot to give Tom a sign for each pitch. Finally, Tom called out to him from the mound, "Get your ass out here, Boomer." Boomer trundled out under the weight of his gear. Stood there, a bad child. Tom snapped at him, "Put some fucking numbers down!" Boomer, puffed up in his drug-fueled bravado, said, "If you're so goddamned good, you won't need any signs." Tom said, "OK with me, you gotta catch them."

I interrupt Tom. "Was he serious?"

"I'm telling the fucking story. Just be quiet and don't ask questions."

"What he'd do if he was guessing fastball and you threw a slider?"

"Not my problem. Will you just listen? I'm building a story here. In creative writing you got to set the reader up for the…the…"

"The climax and the denouement." Tom nods. I say, "So what happened?"

"I'm trying to tell you, but you keep interrupting."

"Did you win the game?"

Tom throws up his hands in frustration and exhales a great breath. "Awright. You win. Yes, I won the game."

"End of story."

Tom glares at me.

After Kelley leaves, Tom and I talk for a while about pitching. He asks me to show him what my pitching motion was like fifty-four years ago. "Do you still remember it?" he says.

"Yes. I can still see it. I just don't know if I can do it. The balance is the bitch when you get old. Standing on one leg with the other leg high in the air."

Tom goes behind me and puts his hands on my waist. "Go ahead," he says, "I'll hold you."

So I go into my motion, turn sideways to an imaginary plate, raise my two hands over my head, then raise my left leg… I begin to wobble on my planted right leg.

Tom holds me tighter around the waist to stabilize me. He says, "Higher." So I raise my left leg higher until it's almost above my head.

Then I lunge forward and down to deliver my electric fastball, with Tom still holding my waist so I don't fall over.

After my pitch, Tom nods, and says, "I can see how hard it must have been for you to duplicate that motion every pitch. So much room for error." He adds, "I would have tightened it up a little for you…" he grins at me, "…if you woulda let me."

"Let you? You're Tom Fucking Seaver, the greatest. YOU, I woulda listened to."

We both laugh.

When it's time to go, I thank Tom for letting me visit him. "I had fun," I say. "Like always."

"I can't believe the way I've been talking today," he says.

We shake hands and I get in my car. Tom stands by my window. Then he leans over to get closer to me. He says, with wonder, "You know, I can still see every pitch."

EPILOGUE
2019

The second decade of the twenty-first century has not been kind to my friend Tom Seaver.

I called Tom in 2014. He clicked onto my call but said nothing. I said, "Tom, it's me."

"Who is this?"

"Jordan."

"What do you want?"

"Just checkin' in, Big Guy. It's been a while." I waited. Then I said, "How are your babies? You in the vineyards now?"

He hung up. I thought his cell phone had dropped the call. I called him back. No answer. A few days later I mailed him a hand-written note. He didn't respond. I complained to Susie, "He can be such a self-centered bastard some times."

She said, "Why should it bother you?"

"I don't know. But it does." So I gave Tom his distance for a few years.

In 2017, I saw on TV news that wildfires were threatening the Napa Valley vineyards. A map of the raging fires came up on the TV screen. A red cloud on the map covered the town of Calistoga. I called

Tom again but got his answering machine. I left a message. "Tom, it's me. Are you and Nancy all right? Are the fires near your vineyards? Call me. Let me know you're OK." But he never called.

After the fires were extinguished, I read a small article in the *New York Daily News* that mentioned that the Napa Valley wildfires had threatened the vineyards and home of Tom Seaver, once a famous baseball pitcher with the New York Mets. The article said that Seaver and his wife Nancy had loaded their truck with Tom's most precious treasures and fled their home. Seaver took his Diebenkorn paintings, photographs of himself in uniform, his prized baseballs, but not his three dogs. He was quoted as saying, "I put them in a place that was safe." That didn't sound like Tom. He loved his dogs. He told me once that as a boy in Fresno he slept with his dogs on cold California nights. "They kept me warm," he said. Nancy, however, wouldn't have his three dogs in their Calistoga house.

No one knew where the Seavers had fled to. A few days later, they surfaced in a hotel room not far from their home. Tom was quoted in that story, saying, "We literally ran like hell." Luckily, his vineyards had been spared. But if they hadn't been spared, Tom said, "The roots are not going to die, just as our roots are not going to die." A facile quote, masked as introspection. Not typical of Tom. It smoked of rewrite, as if someone had fed it to him.

Accompanying that story was a photo of Tom and Nancy inspecting their vineyards after they had returned home. Nancy was still beautiful, with her blonde hair, dark-lensed designer sunglasses, a black sweater, and slacks. She looked like a movie star. She was reaching up her hand to touch the leaves on a vine. Tom was off to her right, behind her, leaning back. He was wearing a trucker's cap, a work shirt, a quilted vest, and his jeans. He bore only a faint resemblance to the Tom Seaver I had last seen at his home in 2013. His hair had turned gray. He had gained weight. His face was puffy. His eyes had the blank, distant, and uncomprehending stare of a confused old man. He was seventy-three.

Two years later, in March 2019, Nancy informed the media that her husband had dementia and was retiring from public life. Nancy, described by Tom's friends as "the Power Behind the Throne," may have been forced to reveal her husband's dementia by a male friend of her daughter Sarah, who had visited the Seavers in 2016. He had taken a photograph of Tom in the vineyards with that same uncomprehending look in his eyes. Then he posted it online for the world to see.

Shortly after Nancy revealed Tom's dementia, the Mets announced that at their June 2019 celebration of the fifty years since the Mets' World Series Championship, they would honor Tom Seaver by renaming 126th Street that led to Citi Field "41 Seaver Way." That ceremony would be held on June 27 at 11:00 a.m. On June 29 at 4:10 p.m., before a Mets-Braves game, the Mets would welcome back "the legends" of their 1969 World Series Championship, such as Cleon Jones and Ron Swoboda and Art Shamsky. Tom would be represented by his two daughters and his grandchildren. Tom, the only true "legend" on that team, and Nancy would not be there.

At some point during this four-day celebration, Jeff Wilpon, the Mets' COO, announced that a bronze statue of Tom would be commissioned for Citi Field. The statue would be between 9 feet and 12 feet tall. Nancy had been lobbying for such a statue for years. She said, "It's ridiculous…. I'm embarrassed for the Mets [for not commissioning such a statue]." But it hadn't been commissioned yet. No artist had been named to create it. Wilpon said that the statue would be erected in a year, or two, maybe longer.

"That statue was long overdue," Marty Appel told me. "Now the statue was happening because Tom wouldn't even know about it. With his dementia, the Mets knew he couldn't come back for the reunion.

They never wanted him back. The only guy who really mattered to that fiftieth-year celebration wouldn't be there."

"It was all so sad," said George Grande over the phone to me. George used to broadcast Yankee games with Tom in 1989. "Tom and I were really close until about 2010. These last four years I have contact only with Nancy now. We all saw it coming. We never believed that Lyme disease story. He'd lost that steely look in his eyes years ago. At one Hall of Fame ceremony, he couldn't read from his script. He said it was because he needed his glasses. Even with his glasses he couldn't read it. But all his friends would tell him, 'Aw, Tom, we're all getting old, we all forget things.' But we knew it was something else. A cylinder was not firing."

I told George that I'd done the same thing with Tom in 2013, when he couldn't remember what I'd eaten for breakfast right in front of him. I'd even lied to him about my superior fastball. Maybe I didn't have a better fastball than Tom Seaver after all, I'd told Tom. We were old men now. Tom was worried about his health. So I'd deferred to my friend. A small price to pay for that friendship that had once been founded on the mutually unshakeable egos of two combative young men.

I heard George Grande's voice over the phone. "We all did that, too, Pat. We all protected him." Then George told me a story:

"One afternoon in '89, after we broadcast a Yankee day game, Tom and I were leaving the stadium. This guy caught our attention. He didn't look like a typical fan in a T-shirt and shorts. He was nicely attired, like he'd gotten dressed for a special occasion. He came walking toward us like he was on a mission. Tom usually just keeps walking when approached by fans, but this time he stopped. The guy was in his forties. He said to Tom, very seriously, 'Mr. Seaver, I want you to know I got every Topps card ever made of you.' Tom was impressed. Then they guy said, 'And recently I sold them all.' Tom looked at me and said, 'Can you believe this guy?

Sold them all! That's crazy.' Tom was obviously annoyed. Then the guy said, 'I recently got married. And I used all the money I got for your cards as a down payment on our first house.' Tom reflected on that for a moment. I will never forget the look on Tom's face. Frozen in time for me. 'Imagine that,' Tom said. He had tears in his eyes."

George paused for a moment, then said, "Tom's heart was even bigger than his body."

"I know," I said. "I miss him."

About the Author

Pat Jordan is an accomplished sports writer and former minor league baseball player. He is a regular contributor to the *New York Times Magazine*, among other periodicals, and his work has been included in *Best American Sports Writing*, *Best American Mystery Stories*, *Best American Essays*, and *Norton Anthology of World Literature*. He is also the author of numerous books, including the memoirs, *A False Spring* and *A Nice Tuesday*.